DARKNESS OVER DENMARK

Hiding below deck, a Danish Jew escapes to Sweden in October 1943.

DARKNESS OVER DENMARK

THE DANISH RESISTANCE AND THE RESCUE OF THE JEWS

ELLEN LEVINE

HOLIDAY HOUSE / NEW YORK

In memory of my father, Nathan Levine
And for Anne, who loves Tivoli

Library of Congress Cataloging-in-Publication Data
Levine, Ellen.
Darkness over Denmark: the Danish resistance and the rescue of the Jews / by Ellen Levine.
p.   cm.
Includes bibliographical references and index.
Summary: An account of people in Denmark who risked their lives to protect and rescue
their Jewish neighbors from the Nazis during World War II.
ISBN 0-8234-1447-7
1. Jews—Persecutions—Denmark Juvenile literature.
2. Holocaust, Jewish (1939–1945)—Denmark Juvenile literature.   3. World War, 1939–1945—
Jews—Rescue—Denmark Juvenile literature.   4. Denmark—History—German occupation,
1940–1945 Juvenile literature.   5. Denmark—Ethnic relations Juvenile literature.
[1. Jews—Persecutions—Denmark.   2. Holocaust, Jewish (1939–1945)—
Denmark.   3. World War, 1939–1945—Jews—Rescue—Denmark.
4. Denmark—History—German occupation,
1940–1945.]   I. Title.   DS135.D4L4   2000
940.53'18'09489—dc21   99–25607
CIP

PHOTO CREDITS

Museet for Danmarks Frihedskamp (The Museum of Danish Resistance), 1940–1945: jacket, bottom;
pp. ii, 3, 4, 11, 31, 33, 34, 38, 40, 56, 67, 71, 83, 97, 106, 113 (both), 114, 118, 119, 133, 140, 141, 142, 143, 159

The New York Public Library, Astor, Lenox, Tilden Foundations: jacket, top

Courtesy of Lui Beilin: p. 147

Courtesy of Salli Besiakov: pp. 77, 129, 147

Courtesy of Miriam (Ruben) and Bent Bograd: pp. 147, 150

Courtesy of Dr. Robert Dean: pp. 80, 149

Courtesy of Birgit Krasnik Fischermann: pp. 95, 148

Courtesy of Jørgen Kieler: pp. 105, 148

Courtesy of Anne Koedt: p. 149

Courtesy of Inger Koedt: pp. 13, 49, 74, 149, 150

Courtesy of Johan Legarth: pp. 54, 148

Courtesy of Jens Ørbeg: p. 9

Courtesy of Tage Seest: pp. 47 (all), 144, 151

Courtesy of Morten Thing: pp. 58, 89, 150, 151

Courtesy of Leif Vidø: pp. 44, 151

Courtesy of Leif and Edith Wassermann: p. 151

Courtesy of Salo Wassermann: pp. 100, 151

CONTENTS

NOTE TO THE READER

THIS IS A DAVID AND GOLIATH STORY. Less than a year after the start of World War II in September 1939, Denmark was invaded by Germany, the country with the most powerful war machine in the world. For five years, the Nazis occupied this small country under the pretense of protecting it from an invasion by England and France.

According to Hitler's racist theories, the Danes were a pure Aryan people, like the Germans. The Nazis called the invaded country a "model protectorate." British prime minister Winston Churchill called it Hitler's "pet canary."

Resistance grew slowly in Denmark, but by the summer of 1943, a crisis loomed. In the face of daily acts of sabotage, the Germans declared a state of emergency and imposed martial law. A month later, they suddenly decided to arrest all of Denmark's Jews and transport them to concentration camps. But, for the first and only time in Nazi Germany's brief history, a large-scale attack on the Jews failed. Danes by the thousands refused to accept that fate for their fellow countrymen. The Jews were, after all, Danes. Whether friends or strangers, they were their neighbors. By resisting, the Danes saved the lives of nearly all of the 8,000 Jews in Denmark.

This is Denmark's story.

PREFACE

SOMETHING UNUSUAL HAPPENED IN DENMARK during World War
II: Hitler's plans to kill the Danish Jews failed. Like many American Jews,
I grew up hearing stories of how Denmark saved its Jews. That Denmark
chose to protect its Jews was an astonishing and extraordinary act. What
happened, and why did it happen in Denmark and nowhere else?

Edmund Burke, the eighteenth-century English political philoso-
pher and member of Parliament, wrote, "The one condition necessary
for the triumph of evil is that good men do nothing." I believe that is
the essence of this story. Evil did not triumph in Denmark because
most Danes simply refused to allow it.

There were "good people" in countries throughout Europe who
helped Jews during the Nazi period. But many more, when faced with
the arrest and murder of their Jewish neighbors, said, "What could we
do?" For Danes, one additional word made all the difference: "What
else could we do?"

To explain what happened in Denmark, historians cite all sorts of
reasons from geography to timing to politics to demographics:

- Denmark was close to neutral Sweden, which could offer a safe
haven.
- The Germans waited for three years before they went after the
Jews in Denmark.
- Some high-placed Germans in Denmark opposed the action
against the Jews.
- The Germans were less brutal in their occupation of Denmark
than in other countries.
- There were fewer than 8,000 Jews in Denmark.

Although all of these factors are true, they primarily explain the success of the rescue. In the end the question remains: Why did Danes act the way they did? I do not know the full answer. I only know that in Denmark Jews were not defined as "the other." Atrocities occur when people are obsessed by their differences. Danes are not saints. There were indeed Danish Nazis. But for the most part, Denmark was a civil—in the fullest sense of the word—society. People respected one another's differences and seemed to care more about ordinary decency than abstract ideals.

I wanted to tell the story of the Danish resistance and rescue in part through the people who experienced it. In the end, the truth is richer than any made-up story, and so true accounts are presented here. I interviewed dozens of people in Denmark and America. All but two of the interviews were conducted in English. These two people were considerably more comfortable speaking Danish, and friends then translated for me. Everyone whose story is included reviewed his or her sections for accuracy. I've changed several names: "Jens" in Chapter 8; "Knud," "Emmy Johansen," and "Erik Jensen" in Chapter 10. I did not interview the first three. They were mentioned in the stories told to me by others. Erik Jensen's name is changed for reasons of privacy. But he wanted me to assure readers that he exists and stands by his story.

I am indebted to those whose stories are told here. In the many hours we spent talking, these most generous people shared their memories, feelings, and their sense of social and political decency. Several extended themselves even beyond the interviews: Salli Besiakov "talked" with me via e-mail several times a week after I returned to New York, sending me fascinating additional gems of information; Anne Koedt interrupted her own work to translate books and magazines whenever I needed them; Inger Koedt was "on call" for dozens of additional "clarifying" conversations. And I miss Bob Koedt, a good friend, who talked with me at length about Denmark and the war before he died in 1992. I wish I had had the chance to share my research with him.

There are many other people to whom I'm deeply indebted: Birte

Peschcke-Køedt; Morten Thing; Jørgen Zahle and his wife, Bente; Professor Therkel Straede; Dr. Robert B. Dean; and Professor Felix Kolmer, a Jewish Czechoslovakian survivor of the Theresienstadt and Auschwitz concentration camps, who was my extraordinary tour guide at Theresienstadt.

I am most grateful to Regina Griffin, my editor, who was always encouraging, always enthusiastic during the many long months of research and writing. I would also like to acknowledge the generous and warm support of everyone at Holiday House, in particular, Claire Counihan, Paula Singer, Lisa Hopp, and of course John and Kate Briggs.

Many others helped, suggesting contacts, translating, and passing on any and all books and materials they thought would be useful: Knud and Alice Asbjørn Smitt; Dori Brenner; Peg Culver; Lauren Friedman; Aviva Futorian; Bill Gross; Mada Liebman; Betty Miles; Charles Nydorf; Jens Ørberg; Ditter Peschcke-Køedt; Grej Peschcke-Køedt; Elinor Robinson; Cindy Seligmann; Toby Yuen; and the members of my writers' group—Bonnie Bryant, Miriam Cohen, Sandra Jordan, Peter Lerangis, Fran Manushkin, Harry Mazer, Norma Fox Mazer, Barbara Seuling, and Marvin Terban.

Finally, I would like to thank Leif H. Rosenstock, photo archivist of the Danish Resistance Museum; and the Royal Danish Embassy and Lis M. Frederiksen, Head of Information, for their continued interest and most generous support of my research.

WHO'S WHO

These are the Danes whose stories are told throughout the book. I interviewed each of these people (some in the United States, most in Denmark), with the exception of Dora Recht and Børge Thing, whose son Morten Thing told me their stories. This quick-reference list shows how old they were at the time of the Nazi invasion of Denmark, April 9, 1940.

LUI BEILIN: 21 years old

SALLI BESIAKOV: 11 years old

BENT BOGRATSCHEW: 5 years old

LEO GOLDBERGER: almost 10 years old

ERIK JENSEN: 12 1/2 years old

JØRGEN KIELER: 21 years old

BIRGIT KRASNIK: 2 years old

JOHAN LEGARTH: 16 years old

EBBA LUND: 16 1/2 years old

ANNE PESCHCKE-KØEDT: 14 months old

BOBS PESCHCKE-KØEDT: 28 years old

BONNIE PESCHCKE-KØEDT: 3 years old

INGER PESCHCKE-KØEDT: 25 years old

RENÉ PESCHCKE-KØEDT: 19 years old

DORA RECHT (THING): 20 years old

MIRIAM RUBEN: 2 years old

TAGE SEEST: 20 years old

BØRGE THING: 23 years old

LEIF VIDØ: 17 years old

LEIF WASSERMANN: 2 years old

SALO WASSERMANN: 15 years old

*"Each time a man stands up for an ideal,
or the lot of others, or strikes out against injustice,
he sends forth a tiny ripple of hope."*
Robert F. Kennedy

*"The struggle of men against power
is the struggle of memory
against forgetting."*
Milan Kundera,
*The Book of Laughter
and Forgetting*

∼

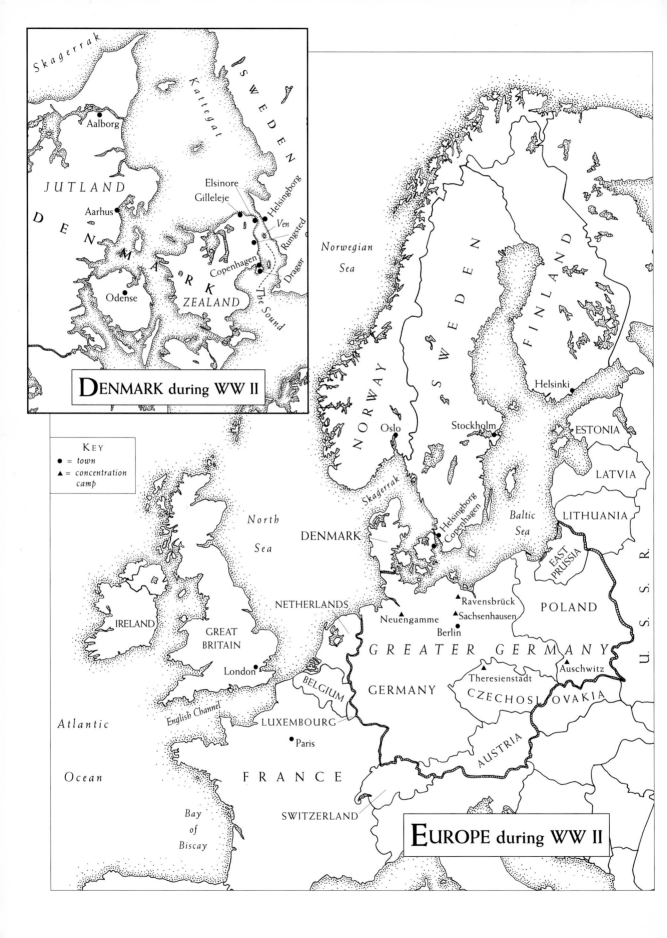

DENMARK during WW II

Skagerrak
Kattegat
SWEDEN
Aalborg
JUTLAND
Elsinore
Gilleleje
Helsingborg
Aarhus
DENMARK
Ven
Rungsted
Copenhagen
Odense
Dragør
ZEALAND
The Sound

KEY
● = town
▲ = concentration camp

Norwegian
Sea

NORWAY
SWEDEN
FINLAND

Helsinki

Oslo
Stockholm
ESTONIA

North
Sea

LATVIA

Skagerrak
Helsingborg
Copenhagen
Baltic
Sea
LITHUANIA

DENMARK

EAST
PRUSSIA

IRELAND
GREAT
BRITAIN

NETHERLANDS
▲ Ravensbrück
Neuengamme ▲ Sachsenhausen
Berlin

POLAND

U.S.S.R.

London

GREATER GERMANY

▲
Theresienstadt
Auschwitz ●

English Channel
BELGIUM
GERMANY
CZECHOSLOVAKIA

Atlantic

LUXEMBOURG
● Paris

AUSTRIA

Ocean

FRANCE

Bay
of
Biscay

SWITZERLAND

EUROPE during WW II

ONE

THE NINTH
OF APRIL

Bent Bogratschew was five years old when German planes flew over Copenhagen on the ninth of April, 1940. Awakened by the noise, he and his sister, who was three years older, ran into his parents' bedroom. They all went out onto the balcony and stared up at the planes. To Bent they looked like huge black birds, a sky full of them. Pieces of paper floated down from the planes. Mr. Bogratschew picked one up and read it.

What was this, Bent wanted to know. His father said quietly, "This is our enemy."

~

The Germans had been planning the invasion of Denmark and Norway for many months. On March 1, 1940, shortly before the attack, Hitler issued a directive about the plan. Labeled "Most Secret, Top Secret," he wrote:

> On principle, we will do our utmost to make the operation appear as a peaceful occupation, the object of which is the military protection of the neutrality of the Scandinavian States. . . . If, in spite of this, resistance should be met, all military means will be used to crush it.[1]

Two days before the invasion, on Sunday, April 7, 1940, a high German military officer, General Kurt Himer, arrived in Copenhagen, Denmark's capital city. Disguised in civilian clothes, he had come to check out last minute details for the secret arrival of a German troopship at Langelinie Pier in the center of the city. It was the perfect place—near the headquarters of the Danish army and close to Amalienborg Castle, where King Christian X and the royal family lived.

Then on April 9, 1940, before dawn, a merchant ship that usually carried coal docked at Langelinie Pier. It sailed by Danish security forces, who barely noted its arrival. Inside the coal ship, however, there was no coal. Instead, like the legendary Trojan horse, soldiers emerged from the cargo areas and spread throughout the city.

Denmark is a small country, made up of some 500 islands (about a hundred of which are occupied) and Jutland, a peninsula that borders Germany and separates the North Sea from the Baltic Sea. The Germans had left nothing to chance—the invasion of Denmark covered the whole country. Planes dropped paratroopers at several different sites, and at four A.M. German troops marched into Jutland.

Twenty minutes later, Cecil von Renthe-Fink, the German ambassador to Denmark, handed the Danish foreign minister an ultimatum announcing that German forces were taking over "the protection" of Denmark. The Germans also announced they would bomb Denmark mercilessly if the Danish government did not accept the occupation. German planes flying over the city confirmed the threat.

At the Jutland border and at Amalienborg Castle, Danish military and royal guards briefly fought the German troops. Gunshots echoed from the palace courtyard, and German bombers circled overhead as the king and his ministers met inside. The commander-in-chief of the Danish armed forces urged the government to reject the German demands and to fight. But armed resistance, others persuasively argued, would mean total devastation. Denmark, with not quite four and a half million people, was no match for Germany, some seventy-five million strong. Denmark's military forces would be overwhelmed by the powerful German war machine in no time at all, these leaders believed. And finally, unlike mountainous Norway, the very flatness of Denmark would have made it impossible to carry out any serious counterattack against the German forces.

Denmark was important to Germany's war strategy for practical

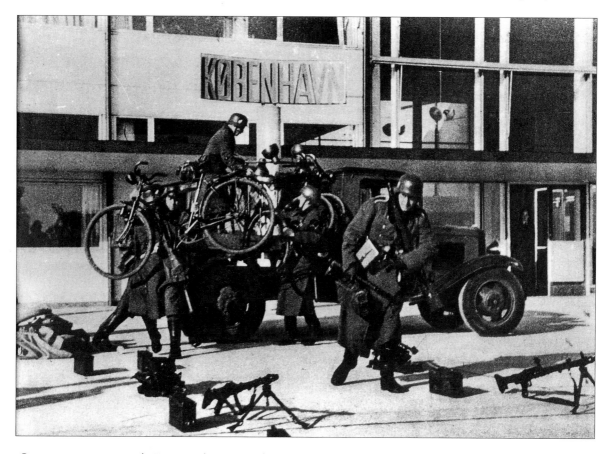

German troops invade Denmark on April 9, 1940.

reasons. In addition, Hitler believed the Danes were perfect Aryans. The small country provided railroad lines to transport Swedish war materials to Germany; it also served as a geographic buffer zone between Britain (and possible Allied attacks) and Germany and was a stepping-stone to Norway; perhaps most important of all, Denmark's rich farming lands were a larder for Germany, feeding millions of Germans their butter, pork, and beef. And so the Nazis wanted "a peaceful occupation" in Denmark.

At the time of the invasion, the Germans assured the Danish government and the king that they would respect Denmark's political independence and would not dissolve the government. The Danish government, believing that fighting would only bring about the com-

A girl reads King Christian X's announcement of Denmark's capitulation to Germany.

plete destruction of the country, wanted to believe all these assurances. At six A.M., less than two hours after the invasion, Denmark, under protest, agreed to Germany's terms, and the king ordered an end to all fighting. For the first time in 900 years, Denmark was no longer a free and independent country.

At the moment of capitulation, the Danish government began what was in effect a policy of cooperation with the German occupying forces. One major exception was Henrik Kauffmann, the Danish ambassador to the United States. He immediately announced that, since the Danish government was now controlled by the Germans, he would not follow any orders from that government. He said he would act in what he considered to be Denmark's true interests. He was officially dismissed from his post, but the United States continued to recognize him as Denmark's "free" ambassador.

In addition to Kauffmann, another group of Danes who were outside the country joined the fight against Germany. Some 5,000 seamen, about ninety percent of the men working on Danish merchant ships, ignored direct orders from their government to return to neutral ports and chose instead to sail with the Allied forces. At home, most Danes accepted their government's decision to accede to Germany's demands—at least at the beginning.

Denmark was accustomed to peace. It had not been involved in any wars since the mid-1800s. In fact, Denmark had been neutral during World War I. Wishing to repeat that experience, the government had signed a non-aggression pact with Germany in 1939, which stated, "The Kingdom of Denmark and the German Reich will in no case resort to war or any other use of force against each other."

The early morning invasion had thus taken Denmark by surprise. Perhaps it shouldn't have, for Danish newspapers had published numerous stories on events in Germany and the rest of Europe. Like much of the world, Danes had watched Germany swallow up Austria, Czechoslovakia, and then Poland.

Danes, like others, also knew that in addition to German military aggression, anti-Semitism was central to Nazi ideology. Even before he came to power, Adolf Hitler had made clear his strongly held anti-Semitic beliefs. In a letter written in 1919, he stated there must be a "systematic legal campaign against the Jews. . . . But the final objective must be the complete removal of the Jews."[2] In *Mein Kampf* ("My Struggle"), Hitler's 1924 autobiography, he wrote, "Was there any form of filth or profligacy, particularly in cultural life, without at least one Jew involved in it? If you cut even cautiously into such an abscess, you find, like a maggot in a rotting body, often dazzled by the sudden light—a kike!"*

It was not surprising then, that when the Nazis first came to power in Germany in 1933, they issued a series of anti-Jewish decrees. All Jews working for federal, state, and local government offices lost their jobs. They were not permitted to work for newspapers, magazines, or radio stations; and they were not allowed to be farmers, teachers, or have anything to do with theater or film.

Then in September 1935, the notorious Nuremberg Laws were

*An insulting term for a Jew.

enacted to further persecute the Jews. They deprived Jews of citizenship and voting rights, and prohibited them from hiring German women as workers. One of the Nuremberg Laws was titled "Law for the Protection of German Blood and Honor." Since the Nazis believed Jewish blood was different from German blood, under this law Jews were forbidden to marry Germans.

Over the next several years, more than a dozen additional decrees were issued. Jews were forbidden to work as doctors or lawyers, or in any of the professions. They were forced to pay huge fines and taxes; and their homes, bank accounts, and other property were taken.

Jews were no longer allowed to butcher animals and prepare meat according to Jewish religious law. They were even forbidden from walking in certain areas of cities. Jewish children were prohibited from attending schools, and signs in many offices and shop windows read "Jews strictly forbidden." As a result, Jews, particularly in smaller towns, often had a hard time finding food. In September 1938, they were forced to carry special identification cards, and their passports were marked with a *J* for *Jude*, the German word for Jew.

Then on the evening of November 9, 1938, a ferocious anti-Jewish riot started in Germany that lasted for two days. Nearly 400 synagogues were burned. Jews were thrown from buses and trains, humiliated, and beaten. Nearly a hundred were killed, and more than 30,000 were arrested and sent to prison camps. Cemeteries and community centers were vandalized and destroyed, and Jewish homes were broken into and looted. Thousands of businesses were devoured in flames, while German fire brigades stood by and watched. German police not only refused to stop the carnage, many actively participated in it.

This infamous event became known as *Kristallnacht*—"Night of Broken Glass." The terrible roar of this German brutality was heard around the world. Less than three months later, Hitler hinted at his future plans. In a speech to the German parliament on January 30, 1939, he thundered that if there was a world war, it would lead to "the destruction of the Jewish race in Europe."

☆ ☆ ☆

Danes considered themselves lucky to have avoided much of the devastation of World War I. So in spite of all the warnings and signs—the blatant military aggression and the hate-filled Nazi propaganda—government leaders and ordinary people, not only in Denmark but also around the world, averted their eyes so as not to see the German war machine as it readied for action.

Seven months after Hitler's speech about Europe's Jews, on September 1, 1939, German troops invaded Poland, and World War II began. On April 9, 1940, Danes could no longer avert their eyes.

〜

Ebba Lund stirred in her sleep. She opened her eyes, yawned, and wondered what was making that steady, droning sound. She looked at the clock. It was much too early, and there was still time before she had to get ready for school. She rolled over and fell back asleep.

Later that morning riding her bike down a Copenhagen street, Ebba was startled to see a crowd of Danes surrounding a small group of German soldiers who looked to Ebba as if they were covered in coal dust. Everyone stared at the soldiers. It seemed like a strange theatrical play. What were they doing here, and why were they carrying arms?

She stopped for a moment to watch. A young man next to her murmured, "I just can't believe it."

"What's happened?" Ebba asked.

"We've been occupied!"

Ebba was stunned. Did this mean Denmark was now part of the war? She took a small detour and rode past the British embassy. A crowd had gathered across the street. As Ebba stood with the others, several trucks with German soldiers pulled up to the curb. The soldiers entered the building and were herding people out and onto the trucks. Someone in the crowd murmured, "They're taking the diplomatic personnel." Someone else yelled, "Hurrah for the Britons!" Others picked up the chant.

A piercing command momentarily silenced the onlookers: "Anyone attempting to escape will be shot!" The crowd shifted uneasily and stared at the trucks filling up with people. Then almost as one, everyone again shouted, "Hurrah for the Britons! Hurrah for the Britons!"

~

Leo Goldberger listened to the drone of the planes. Staring out the window of his family's Copenhagen apartment, he watched as thousands of green leaflets fell from German aircraft. He reached through the open window and grabbed one. It was hard to read, for it was written in a strange mixture of Danish, German, and Norwegian. "OPROP!" the headline screamed. "ATTENTION!" The leaflet was addressed to the "Danish Soldiers and the Danish People." The Germans had come to protect the Danes from the evil plans of the English and the French. All Danes should go on with their lives as if everything was normal.

Leo awakened his parents. His father, one of the chief cantors for the congregation at Copenhagen's main synagogue, became extremely upset. And Leo understood that what was happening was anything but "normal."

When Leo was four years old in 1934, his parents had emigrated to Denmark from Czechoslovakia, where they had worried about a possible Nazi takeover of their city. Leo remembered a story his father had told him. One day a group of young Nazis had stopped an old Jewish man in the street. They scoffed at him, sneering and yelling. They tore at his beard and finally spat on him. Leo's father still felt anger and revulsion when he remembered the scene. Leo knew that was when his father had begun to look for a job elsewhere. It had seemed a small miracle to come to peaceful, safe Copenhagen. But now, now what would happen?

OPROP!

Til Danmarks Soldater og Danmarks Folk!

Uten Grund og imot den tyske Regjerings og det tyske Folks oprigtige Ønske, om at leve i Fred og Venskab med det engelske og det franske Folk, har Englands og Frankrigets Magthavere ifjor i September erklæret Tyskland Krigen.

Deres Hensigt var og blir, efter Mulighet, at treffe Afgjørelser paa Krigsskuepladser som ligger mere afsides og derfor er mindre farlige for Frankriget og England, i det Haab, at det ikke vilde være mulig for Tyskland, at kunde optræde stærkt nok imot dem.

Af denne Grund har England blandt andet stadig krænket Danmarks og Norges Nøitralitæt og deres territoriale Farvand.

Det forsøkte stadig at gjøre Skandinavien til Krigsskueplads. Da en yderlig Anledning ikke synes at være givet efter den russisk-finnske Fredsslutning, har man nu officielt erklæret og truet, ikke mere at taale den tyske Handelsflaates Seilads indenfor danske Territorialfarvand ved Nordsjøen og i de norske Farvand. Man erklærte selv at vilde overta Politiopsigten der. Man har tilslut truffet alle Forberedelser for overraskende at ta Besiddelse af alle nødvendige Støtepunkter ved Norges Kyst. Aarhundredes største Krigsdriver, den allerede i den første Verdenskrig til Ulykke for hele Menneskeheden arbeidende Churchill, uttalte det aapent, at han ikke var villig til at la sig holde tilbake af »legale Afgjørelser eller nøitrale Rettigheder som staar paa Papirlapper«.

Han har forberedt Slaget mot den danske og den norske Kyst. For nogen Dage siden er han blit utnævnt til foransvarlig Chef for hele den britiske Krigsføring.

This leaflet dropped by German aircraft exhorts Danes to accept German occupation for their own "protection" from the English and French.

TWO

THE OCCUPATION

THE GERMANS HAD EXPECTED TO CONQUER Denmark quickly, and they did. The Danish air force was destroyed before any planes had a chance to leave the ground. In the brief fighting that took place, thirteen Danish soldiers were killed and twenty-three wounded. The navy had no casualties, for no Danish ships opened fire on German ships. By breakfast on April 9, the country was no longer a free and independent nation.

The Danish government explained its rapid capitulation in a public proclamation:

> The Government has acted in the honest conviction that in so doing we have saved the country from an even worse fate. It will be our continued endeavor to protect our country and its people from the disasters of war, and we shall rely on the people's cooperation.

Although most Danes were anti-German and anti-Nazi, in the first years of the occupation, they supported the government's position as necessary to avoid open warfare. For many, this "policy of negotiation," as some called it, seemed to work. Daily life was hardly affected at first. The government, the courts, and the Danish police remained in power. Businesses operated with little change, and children went to school as they always had. In the beginning of the occupation, there were scarcely any shortages.

Within days of the occupation, King Christian resumed his morning horseback ride through the streets of Copenhagen. He ignored German soldiers when they saluted him, but responded to the greetings of Danes. The king rode alone, to the surprise of the

In a small but powerful act of defiance, King Christian X rides his horse through the streets of Copenhagen during the occupation.

Germans, who always saw their Führer protected by security guards.

"Who guards the king?" they asked the Danes.

"We all do," was the answer.

∼

During the occupation, when Leo Goldberger walked to school, he often saw the king on his morning ride. He delighted in looking at the crisp uniform, with its double row of shining buttons. The king was always in uniform, and always wore a small military hat. He rode the same route every day and always at the same time.

Before the war when Leo had first seen the king riding, like most Danish children, he had been thrilled at the sight. Now, with the Germans in his homeland, Leo was comforted. Somehow he knew it was important that the king did this every day. You could almost set your watch by it, it was so regular, he thought. As long as the king was around, things couldn't be that bad.

∼

Even many Danes who before the occupation sometimes had wondered whether Denmark really needed a monarch were comforted by the sight of the elderly king quietly defying the Germans.

It was impossible to live in Denmark after April 9 and not see German soldiers. The soldiers seemed to relish being in Denmark, away from actual warfare. Food was plentiful and delicious, at least in the early years of the occupation, and you could stroll at leisure through Tivoli, the famous amusement park and gardens in Copenhagen. Theaters, museums, restaurants, and cafes were all open for business and thriving.

The Danes quickly became used to the ordinary German soldiers in their brownish green uniforms. They were the "Wehrmacht" (the military), and they were usually polite and well disciplined. Most Danes, including children, were not really afraid of them, although some resented the soldiers.

∼

Every Wednesday morning, Bonnie Peschcke-Køedt would stand with a group of kids on the beach near Elsinore and watch a German soldier row to shore from a boat in the Sound. He'd pull his rowboat up on the sand and then march into the local bakery, carrying a large sack with him. He never looked at the children, who stared in fascination in the beginning and then in anger and frustration as the weeks went by. In the shop he'd sweep all the day-old pastries into his sack. Our pastries! Bonnie thought. Then he'd turn around, march back down to the beach, and row out into the Sound.

∼

The Gestapo and the SS officers, however, were totally different. They were the feared Nazi police and security forces, known for their arrogance and cruelty. Gestapo officials wore black coats and black hats. SS officers also dressed in black, with a skull-and-crossbones insignia on their uniforms.

∼

René Peschcke-Køedt's nickname was Bibber, and everyone called him that. He was nineteen years old on April 9, and it was a day he would never forget. He'd gone into Copenhagen from his family's home in Charlottenlund. There were Germans all over the place. And those damned Donald Ducks! he said to himself. That's what they all called the German hydroplanes that landed in the harbor, for they flew and floated and made a deep, ugly sound. Bibber admired his older brother Bobs. It was clear that Bobs felt anger and contempt for the Germans, but he was calm and so sure of himself

The Peschcke-Køedts. In the back row, far left, stands Bibber, and on the far right, Bobs, with their other brothers and sister.

whenever he encountered them. And he had a great sense of humor, thought Bibber. That's what he really admired.

German troops had taken over an army barracks five minutes away from Bibber's house, where he lived with his parents. Soldiers and officers passed in front of the house day and night. They'd often stop and search you if you were carrying something.

Bobs and his wife, Inger, lived nearby. In ordinary times, it was a quick walk, but the winters during the war were particularly bitter cold. It was bad enough having the Germans occupy your country, Bibber thought, but it seemed as if the weather was conspiring to make it even more miserable.

Bibber's house was large, but his family used only a few of the rooms. There was so little fuel, you simply couldn't heat the whole house. One afternoon Bibber took a sled over to Bobs and Inger's to borrow a sack of coal.

It was late when he started back. It got dark early during the winter, and Bibber lowered his head against the damp cold wind.

"Was ist das?" ("What is that?") demanded the Gestapo officer, as he kicked the bag on the sled.

Bibber hadn't seen the officer in the shadows and was startled. Then he felt irritated. Who was this man? Just because he was German, he thought he had a right to bother people. In a matter of seconds, Bibber's irritation turned to ridicule.

"It's weapons," he said, half-smiling at the officer. Let him look inside the sack, he thought. He'll only find the damn coal.

"Just weapons," he repeated.

The officer looked at Bibber as if he were crazy. I bet he's thinking, These Danes make such stupid jokes. Bibber smiled to himself. The officer stared for a moment, turned, and walked off.

～

Although most Danes accepted their government's policy of accommodating the German invaders, the occupation also reminded them that their country's traditions were different from Germany's. Denmark had a long history of democracy. Its political system was based on principles of not only individual liberty, but also equality—

a belief that everyone in the nation should share social benefits and responsibilities. This for Danes was the meaning of social justice.

But in wartime, could one be certain that people would treasure these values? There are no guarantees in a democracy, except that different voices have a right to be heard. It is so much simpler to let others do your thinking, rather than to struggle yourself to understand all the issues.

There were some Danes who admired the Germans and hoped for a German victory in the war. These Danish Nazis, however, were small in number and despised by the vast majority of Danes. The Danish Nazi political parties, of course, hoped to gain strength with the German invasion and occupation. They staged parades and published newspapers modeled after German anti-Semitic papers.

A Nazi government had taken hold in Germany, and a fascist one in Italy. Both were anti-democratic regimes. Could it happen in Denmark? some people wondered and feared. In the early months of the occupation, a group of young people formed an organization called the Union of Danish Youth. With the help of adults, they sponsored lectures and other cultural events that stressed and celebrated the Danish ideas of democratic nationalism. Hal Koch, a professor of church history at the University of Copenhagen, became perhaps the most important spokesperson for this movement. Koch lectured around the country to packed auditoriums. Democracy and nationalism were not abstract ideas for Koch. He believed that the role of the Union of Danish Youth was "to politicize youth, that is, to arouse interest and spread knowledge regarding the country and public life until a feeling of responsibility has been created." It was almost as if the whole country was engaged in a nationwide conversation.

By late 1942 and into the next year, Danes began to suffer some of the hardships of other European nations. Heating fuel became so scarce, many people chopped up pieces of furniture, or burned peat dug up from bogs and dried. Gasoline was rationed, and cars sat in garages until well after the end of the war. Doctors, ministers, some journalists, and a few others, were the only ones allowed to buy gas. They were in "necessary" professions.

Some taxicabs had contraptions that burned wood or cow dung or peat instead. Small pieces were tossed into the makeshift engine, emitting a foul smell. Most Danes traveled on their bikes. It was not unusual, on a Saturday night, to see people dressed up for a party, pedaling through the streets of the city. At different times during the war, the Germans imposed curfews. If a curfew started at eight P.M., partygoers sometimes took their children with them and stayed at the gathering until the morning hours when the curfew would be lifted.

Wooden clogs became popular, for leather shoes were in limited supply. Knitting yarn was so scarce, people unraveled old sweaters and used that yarn to knit new pieces of clothing. Old socks were mended over and over until hardly anything was left of the original sock.

There was no such thing as real coffee. Coffee drinkers drank a mix made from ground grains or chicory root. There were food shortages, but Danes never starved as people did, for example, in Holland. The government issued ration books, and many items could only be bought with these coupons.

As the war progressed, air raids became more frequent. The wail of the sirens was a terrifying sound. Fire-engine sirens were equally frightening, for they could mean a bomb had exploded nearby. Sometimes air-raid sirens went off as children were on their way to or from school. In a city, if they heard a siren, they knew to head for the nearest public underground air-raid shelter. They sat with strangers, sometimes for hours, waiting for the all-clear signal. Outside the cities, there were few public shelters, and children had different instructions from their parents.

∿

During the week, Bonnie rode her bicycle to a small private school in the suburbs of Copenhagen. There were eleven students in her class, and most of them also biked to school. On the way, she rode through a short tunnel that went under a railroad track.

Bonnie thought about the tunnel whenever she left the house. It was halfway to school and an important landmark. The first day she had ridden alone, Pa had talked to her about air raids. She felt very grown-up knowing that although the bombs were frightening, it was the English who were doing the bombing. And the English were heroes, Pa had said.

If the air-raid siren went off before she reached the tunnel, Pa had told her to turn around and come home. If she had passed through the tunnel, she was to go on to school.

Bonnie pedaled rapidly. It was a gray morning, and she was cold. She leaned down into the wind. Halfway through the tunnel, the siren began to wail. Halfway! What should she do? Pa hadn't covered this. In a flash she decided she'd rather be home when there was trouble. She turned the bike around and pedaled furiously.

When she arrived home safely, she was proud of her decision, and thought Pa would be, too. But for the rest of her life, she always felt slightly sick when she heard a certain siren sound.

∼

Although most Danes supported the government's policy of working with the German occupiers, many people expressed their hostility to the invaders through individual acts of defiance. Ridicule was a common way. One evening at the theater, a Danish comedian looked down at his audience and saw the front rows filled with German officers. They had taken the best seats in the house for themselves. He began his act by snapping his right arm forward as if in a Nazi salute.

The German officers leapt to their feet, saluted the stage, and shouted, "Heil Hitler!" The comedian paused, kept his arm straight out, and said softly, "This is how high the snow was last winter in Copenhagen . . ."

Groups of Danes would gather in public squares and parks and hold *alsangs* (community singing). Most popular were Danish folk and patriotic songs. It was a while before the Germans realized that these group sing-alongs were not simply casual gatherings, but rather a way for Danes to demonstrate a simple form of national unity in the face of the enemy. And then the Germans banned the alsangs.

Teenagers played pranks on German soldiers. We will never know for certain whether all of those reported actually happened. But perhaps even more important, the stories reflect how many people felt about the German invaders in their midst. One story tells of a traffic post the Nazis had set up at a main intersection in Copenhagen. It was a waist-high circle of sandbags, and inside stood a German soldier directing traffic. One morning as the streets filled with people walking and bicycling to work, a laughing crowd surrounded the soldier. Traffic halted and a logjam developed. Finally an SS car arrived. One of the black-uniformed officers got out of the car and tore down a sign on the traffic post that someone had tacked up. It read: "Attention! This soldier is not wearing trousers!"

Other pranks were more dangerous, such as slashing the tires of German cars, or painting the windshields of Nazi vehicles. The letter *V,* the sign for British victory, appeared on fences and walls all over Copenhagen. If caught, the perpetrator would be arrested. In the first years of the occupation, an arrest for a minor incident was probably not too serious. If the Germans made the arrest, they almost always turned the person over to the Danish police and Danish judges, who were often very lenient. In the later years of the war, punishment could be much more serious.

∽

It was such a beautiful afternoon, Inger and three friends decided to bicycle to Hornbaek, a small fishing town in north Zealand. But even on a beautiful day one couldn't forget the Germans. On the way they passed bunkers the soldiers had built along the coastline. Machine-gun mounts faced the water so that the Germans could fire on British planes flying to Sweden or down the coast.

After a walk through the town, at last it was time to go back. The bike path home skirted in and out of the woods, past the Nazi barracks. A garbage dump near the barracks emitted a terrible smell, for it hadn't been cleared in many days. Outside the barracks, two soldiers sat on a bench talking and laughing with several young Danish women.

As they rode by, Inger tilted her head up and dramatically held her nose. One of the soldiers leapt up and shouted "Halt!" The bikes skidded to a stop as the four jammed down on their brakes.

The soldier ran over and grabbed Inger's handlebars. "What were you doing?" he shouted.

"The garbage smells awful," she answered.

He sneered and grabbed her arm. The bike fell to the ground. "Then you'll have to stay here until you get used to the smell!" and he pulled her toward the buildings.

Her friends watched, horrified. They rode off, taking Inger's bike with them. When they saw a public telephone, they called police headquarters in Elsinore and reported Inger's arrest.

At the barracks, Inger was taken to a room and told to sit and wait. It was foolish to have held her nose, she thought. Of course the smell was bad, but that's not why she had done it. She hated that the Germans had taken over her country and felt angry that any Danish women would be friendly toward them. Most of all she was frustrated at not being able to do anything. On an impulse she had made that defiant gesture. Now, she waited.

"I'm here to pick up Inger Peschcke-Køedt," the Danish police officer said to the German soldier. As Inger climbed into the police car, the Danish officer said quietly, "Don't say anything." Loudly, for the Germans to hear, he said to the driver, "Back to headquarters."

As they drove out of sight of the barracks, the officer asked Inger where she lived. To her immense relief, he dropped her at her gate. "Next time be more careful," he said.

～

A year later, in the summer of 1943, Danes arrested for "insulting" German soldiers often were sentenced to time in jail.

THREE
JEWS IN DENMARK

AT THE TIME OF THE GERMAN INVASION, there were around 8,000 Jews in Denmark. Like other Danes, when they awoke to the sound of the planes on April 9, they did not know what to expect. The next day representatives of the Danish Jewish Community, an organized community group, met in Copenhagen. How should Denmark's Jews react?

The Jewish community in Denmark, although small, was not homogeneous.* There were several distinct groups. Recent Jewish immigrants from Germany, Austria, Czechoslovakia, and Poland knew firsthand the viciousness of Nazi policies against the Jews. They had come to Denmark after Hitler had taken power in Germany in 1933. About 1,500 of them were in Denmark that April morning, and they were afraid.

Earlier, after World War I, Jewish refugees from several European countries had made their way to Denmark. Still earlier, at the turn of the century, a few thousand Jews had immigrated to Denmark. Almost all had come from Russia. Young Jewish men, often kidnapped from Russian streets, were forced to serve for twenty-five years in the tsar's army. Many escaped to different European countries, including Denmark. Thousands made their way across the ocean to America.

Other Russian Jews had fled pogroms, terrible riots during which gangs of people, encouraged by local police and sometimes even by church leaders, attacked and murdered Jews. Although violence against Jews was a personal memory for many of these immigrants, life in Denmark had been different. Even now with the German invasion, the Danish government still remained in power, and the Danish king

*The "Jewish Community" with a capital C refers to a specific organization known as the Danish Jewish (sometimes called Mosaic) Community. The phrase "Jewish community" with a lower-case c refers to the Jewish population in general.

was still the monarch. Perhaps Denmark's Jews, like other Danes, would be safe. By April 1940, these Russian and World War I immigrants numbered about 3,400.

And then there were the Viking Jews, as they called themselves, numbering about 1,600, whose families had lived in Denmark for centuries. Their ancestors had come at the invitation of King Christian IV, who in 1622 had promised them freedom of religion and the right to engage in trade. At the time, indeed for generations before that, most Jews had lived under some form of official or governmental discrimination. In 1516 in Venice, for example, the Catholic Church had ordered walls to be built around the Jewish area. At night the gates were closed, and the Jewish inhabitants locked inside. The area was called the "ghetto," and the word is still used today for a segregated living area.

Ghettos were set up throughout western Europe. In eastern Europe Jews lived in isolated towns and villages called shtetls. Although not locked behind walls, they were deliberately kept separated from the rest of the community and suffered from many of the same prejudices as their western European counterparts.

In the ghettos Jews sometimes were forced to wear special items of clothing, or insignia patches sewn onto their clothes. These cities-within-cities existed in most western European countries until the 1800s and the European movements and revolutions for social and political change. By the mid-1800s, ghetto gates were no longer locked.

In Denmark there never were ghettos. In 1814, earlier than in most European countries, Jewish Danes gained full equality. In March of that year, King Frederick VI decreed that,

> . . . those of the Jewish faith who were born in the kingdom of Denmark, or have received permission to settle within its borders, should have equal opportunity with the rest of the citizens to earn a living and support themselves according to the established laws.

Over the next century, the Jewish community became so well

integrated into non-Jewish Danish society that it was in serious danger of disappearing through intermarriage. By 1940 there were at least 1,300 people who were half-Jewish, the children of mixed marriages. This steady absorption into the larger society was slowed by the arrival of the new immigrants who brought with them a strong Jewish identity. At the same time these new immigrants also worked hard at becoming Danes. They learned the Danish language, labored side by side with Danes, enjoyed Danish food, and even began to think of themselves as Danes—Jewish Danes.

There was another group of Jews in Denmark. They were refugees, but not of the usual kind. They were refugees-in-transit. In the 1930s nearly 1,500 young Zionists had come for agricultural training in Denmark on their way to Palestine. They were called *halutzim* (pioneers, in Hebrew). By 1943, some 500 were left in Denmark, trapped by the occupation.

In addition there was a group of younger refugee children. After Kristallnacht in 1938, several women's groups, in particular the Danish Women's League for Peace and Freedom and the Society of Jewish Women, worked to get young Jews out of Germany, first to Denmark, and then to Palestine. The children were called the youth "Aliyah" (emigration to Palestine) or the "League children." In September 1943, there were 174 of them left in the country.

In the years before World War II, Jews in Denmark, unlike Jews in most other lands, experienced little anti-Semitism in their daily lives. The tone was set by the Danish government and the Danish Lutheran Church. For decades both had accepted Jews as equal citizens, while respecting their religious differences. Although some Danish missionary groups had tried to convert the Jews to Christianity, their activities were generally frowned upon by the government and the society as a whole.

Relations between the Danish monarchy and the Jewish community were quite cordial. In the spring of 1933, the Copenhagen synagogue planned to celebrate its hundredth anniversary. It had invited

King Christian X to attend a special service, and he had promised to come. In contrast, in April of that same year, just south of the Danish border, Adolf Hitler declared a national boycott of Jewish stores.

The story is told that the chairman of the Jewish Community asked for an audience with the king. When it was granted, the chairman explained that the Jewish Community would understand if the king decided not to attend the service because of what was happening in Germany. King Christian is reported to have said, "Are you out of your right mind, man? Now, of course, is when I shall be coming."[3] And so a week and a half after Hitler ordered a nationwide boycott against Jews in Germany, King Christian X paid tribute to a hundred years of religious freedom for Jews in Denmark.

In 1936, after a Danish Nazi group published a particularly hate-filled pamphlet, a group of Danish church leaders, including the bishop of Copenhagen, issued a public statement denouncing the publication. Clearly, before the war the Danes did not share the anti-Jewish hatred sweeping their southern neighbor.

Five years later, in the early years of the occupation, Danish clergy again rejected German racism and anti-Semitism. In December 1941, a group of clergymen met to discuss their opposition to the introduction of German racial laws in Denmark. One of the ministers explained to Copenhagen's chief rabbi, Max Friediger, that their support for their Jewish neighbors was inextricably connected to their nationalism. He wrote:

> For us this is not just a question of Jews and their rights, but for us Danes it must first and foremost be a question of a small nation's right to exist, yes, a question of our entire national attitude and of the fundamentals of popular government: equality and human dignity.

Lutheranism is the official religion of Denmark. Yet as one Danish author has written, "[Danes are] not infused with religious fervor. Denmark adopted the Lutheran religion very early after the Reformation as the state religion, but gave religious liberty to all its citizens."[4] Indeed, before the war it was rare for most Jews in Denmark to feel "different" because of being Jewish. And so uncommon was it to categorize people by their religion, that differences, which were in fact religiously based, were not always recognized as such.

~

Salli Besiakov loved to sing. Any chance he could get, he sang. In school he always volunteered for any chorus, and everybody said he had a fine voice. When Salli was nine years old, he and another boy were chosen by the schoolmaster to audition at a special music school in Copenhagen. Salli wanted to be a singer, and he was thrilled at the chance to try out for the school. It was the best place in Copenhagen, perhaps all of Denmark, to study music.

One morning, Salli went for his tryout. As he sat in a hallway waiting his turn, he smiled to himself. The faint sounds of a piano drifted out from the audition room. He couldn't quite make out the tune, but he knew so many songs, he felt confident.

At last it was Salli's turn. In the room one grown-up sat behind a desk, and another at a piano. "Good morning," the pianist said as he smiled at Salli. "I'm going to play a brief introduction and then I want you to join in with the words." The piano teacher began to play, and then nodded for Salli to begin.

Salli listened, surprised. This was a song he didn't know. He shook his head. "I'm sorry, I don't know it," he said.

"That's fine," the other teacher said. "We'll do another one."

Again the piano teacher began. And again Salli was silent. By the third try, his jacket began to weigh heavy on his shoulders, and his hands felt sweaty.

"In the East, the sun rises," the teacher prompted and paused. Salli was silent. " . . . and God's light from the East . . . " The teacher waited, but Salli said nothing. "The star over Bethlehem . . . " the teacher added pointedly.

Still Salli didn't say a word.

"Try another," the desk teacher said to the pianist. "He's probably just nervous."

Salli was confused. These must be church hymns, he thought. But he didn't know them. He was Jewish.

Everybody always said, You have a fine voice, Salli kept telling himself. Now, for the first time in his life, Salli couldn't say a word.

After six tries, the teachers dismissed him. As he closed the door behind him, he heard one of them say, "Not a very bright child. I wonder why they sent him to us."

That was the first time Salli realized that being Danish and Jewish was not the same as being just Danish.

A year later, when Salli was ten, he and his schoolteacher became friends in a most unusual way. And it was because Salli was the only Jewish child in his class.

In November 1939 the Soviet Union invaded Finland. Although Denmark did not become officially involved in the "Winter War," most Danes sided with Finland and found different ways to help. It was an extremely bitter winter, and Finland's food supplies were running low. Organizations throughout Denmark collected money for food packages to send to Finland.

"The children in Finland are starving, and so the school is making a collection," Salli's teacher said one morning. "It doesn't matter how much you bring. Tell your parents and ask them for a donation," he instructed the students.

Salli and his friends didn't know very much about Finland. Denmark, they knew from their history lessons, stayed out of war, and was proud of its traditions of peace and neutrality. Their teacher seemed to think the war between Finland and the Soviet Union was important, but Denmark wasn't at war. So Salli forgot about asking his parents for money.

The next day in class the teacher asked everyone with a donation to bring it to the front of the room. Hardly anyone stepped forward. It seemed most everybody had forgotten.

The teacher became angry. He looked around the room and snapped, "What kind of Jews are you all?"

In his whole life Salli had never heard anyone say anything like that. But without consciously thinking about it, he knew instantly that the teacher was saying "Jew" meant "stingy."

The words had barely left his mouth when the teacher quickly glanced at Salli. Most of the other kids probably didn't know Salli was Jewish. Nobody ever talked about religion. But the teacher knew, and Salli knew. The teacher looked away, and then back again at Salli, who felt trapped in his chair. Why did the teacher keep staring at him?

For a flicker of a moment their eyes locked. Suddenly Salli understood. The teacher felt ashamed! Salli read a silent apology in his eyes.

Salli never mentioned the incident, and neither did his teacher. But from that day on, the teacher always smiled at Salli in a most friendly way. And Salli would smile back.

Four months later, Germany invaded Denmark. Salli listened as his parents and their friends talked about the war. This time Denmark *was* involved, and this time Salli paid attention.

~

What should the official Jewish Community do in light of the German invasion? It was a difficult question for the board of representatives. All Danes, including Jews, worried for their country. But Danish Jews had other fears as well. They knew what was happening in countries under German control. Many of the recent immigrants still had relatives in these countries. As for Denmark, it had always provided a safe haven for the Jews. But would it—could it—now?

Rabbi Marcus Melchior, assistant rabbi of Copenhagen's main synagogue, said Danish Jews took heart when a Jewish professor gave a radio lecture the evening of the occupation. In his autobiography, Rabbi Melchior wrote, " . . . in Denmark, life apparently was to go on more or less as usual. The king was the king, and the Jewish professor was a professor—and radio lecturer! Perhaps, then, after all . . . in the midst of the sinister atmosphere . . . perhaps, perhaps . . ."

Perhaps they might be safe in Denmark.

The Jewish Community Board's goal was to avoid provoking the German authorities. Nothing should be done to give the Nazis an excuse to arrest the Jews. During the first two months of the occupation, they canceled all lectures about Jewish issues and stopped publication of a Jewish family magazine. The board increased its aid for refugees, but "refugee aid" was now called "charity work," so as not to arouse the attention of the Germans. Most important of all, the board agreed to fully support the Danish government's policy of accommodating the Germans. Resistance to the occupation, these Jewish leaders believed, would bring attention to their community, and who knew what dire consequences might result.

The Germans, for their own reasons, decided not to attack Denmark's Jews, at least not in the early years of the occupation. Danish government officials had made clear to the German diplomatic envoy, Minister Renthe-Fink, that anything regarding Danish Jews was a matter of internal Danish government policy and must be left to the Danes. Six days after the occupation began, Renthe-Fink sent a report to Berlin stating that the Danish authorities were concerned lest Germany take steps against Denmark's Jews:

> If we [Germany] do anything more in this respect than is strictly necessary, this will cause paralysis of or serious disturbances in [Danish] political and economic life. The importance of the problem should not therefore be underestimated.

Danish farms supplied large amounts of produce to Germany, and Danish railroad lines had to be kept open for materials shipped to Germany from Norway and Sweden. A peaceful Denmark was vital to Germany. The less trouble the better.

Although the Jewish Community tried to be as invisible as possible, other Danes were not as silent. A year after the occupation began, the Danish chief of police, Thune Jacobsen, had a brief meeting with Heinrich Himmler, head of the feared Nazi SS. When Himmler raised the subject of the "Jewish problem," Jacobsen answered, "The Danish population does not consider this topic a problem." "No Jewish problem" became the catch phrase that described official Danish policy regarding its Jewish population.

In October 1941 Christmas Møller, leader of the Conservative Party, and later one of the leaders of the resistance movement, gave a rousing speech at Hellerup High School in Copenhagen. He attacked the German occupiers and stressed Denmark's democratic traditions. The treatment of Jews in Germany, he said, "is completely unsuitable for the Danish character."

From the beginning of the occupation, the Germans had assured the Danish government that it would remain free and independent. At the same time, the Nazis demanded various concessions from the government about Denmark's military forces, trade agreements, court system, and other areas of public life. In fact, the government had to negotiate continually with the German occupiers. Some demands were rejected, others were reluctantly agreed to. On certain issues, Denmark's political leaders felt they had to draw the line.

In November 1941 the Danish governing council decided that it could not accept any German attempts to introduce anti-Jewish legislation into Denmark as had been done elsewhere. The government's minister of religion assured Copenhagen's chief rabbi there would be no Nuremberg-type laws in Denmark *so long as the government remained in power.*

Two months earlier, in September 1941, Jews in Germany had been forced to wear a yellow Star of David on their clothing to identify them as Jews. Not long after that, the Germans required Jews to wear the yellow star in countries they occupied. But they never tried to introduce this law in Denmark.

There have been many rumors and legends about Denmark and the yellow Star of David. According to one story, when the Germans demanded that Jews wear the star, the entire Danish population wore it. That never happened. In another tale, when the Jews had to wear the star, King Christian was the first to put it on. That also never happened. And in the most frequently repeated story, the king announced that if any Dane had to wear the star, he'd be the first. That, too, never happened.

These myths do, however, reflect a truth about the Danes and their king. The government and the vast majority of the Danish people clearly rejected the rabid anti-Semitic ideas and policies of the Germans. And the Danes believed that whether or not King Christian actually said those words, it would have been like him to express such support for a group of his people.

Nevertheless, the small group of Danish Nazis persisted in their anti-Semitic activities. In late 1941 they increased their attacks on Jews in their leading newspaper. Then, on December 20, in the dark hours of the morning, a man broke into the Copenhagen synagogue and attempted to burn it down. The fire was caught in time, and there was little damage. Less than a month and a half later, the arsonist was convicted and sentenced by a Danish court to serve three years and twenty days in prison. It is remarkable that in wartime Europe in February 1942, in a country occupied by the Nazis whose world plan was to exterminate European Jewry, a man was *convicted and punished* for a crime he committed against Jews.

On New Year's Day 1942, in a note to Rabbi Melchior thanking him for the gift of a book, King Christian expressed his sadness about the attack on the Copenhagen synagogue and his relief that little damage had been done. With this gracious thought from their king, Denmark's Jews began the new year.

FOUR
RESISTANCE BEGINS

IT WAS AS IF THE JEWISH COMMUNITY in Denmark held its breath and waited. To be as invisible as possible was the safest course, many believed. The Danish king and government had been good to them, and so they supported the "policy of negotiation," as did most Danes. The Germans were obviously treating Denmark differently from other occupied countries. Perhaps they would be treated differently from other European Jews.

Although a distinct minority, there were some Danes who believed that anything short of resistance was merely sticking one's head in the sand and ignoring reality. They thought the government should not negotiate with Nazis once the immediate danger of the ninth of April was over. "Negotiation" to their way of thinking meant "collaboration." And although Denmark and Germany were not officially at war, Germany to them was clearly an enemy to be fought. They believed Denmark in time would have to make so many concessions to the German occupiers that the government would be Danish in name only.

From April 1940 until August 1943, the government in fact *was* forced to accept many German demands. As country after country in Europe fell under German control, Hitler became obsessed with the idea of conquering the Soviet Union. Breaking his peace agreement with Stalin, Hitler sent his troops into Russia. The attack, called Operation Barbarossa, began on June 22, 1941. At first the German offensive seemed successful. But the consequences in Denmark were largely unanticipated by the Nazi occupiers.

The Communist Party in Denmark was one of many political parties with elected representatives in the Danish parliament. It was not illegal to be a communist. When Germany declared war against the Soviet Union, Hitler demanded that the Danish government "declare war" against Danish communists. Danish police arrested communist leaders and active party members, including members of Parliament. More than three hundred people were arrested, some of whom remained in prison for four years. Although some of them were Jews, they were arrested as political enemies of the Nazi regime, not because they were Jews.

Later in 1941, pressured by Germany, the Danish government went even further and outlawed all communist organizations. These actions were a direct violation of the Danish constitution, which stated that no citizen could be arrested for his or her religious or political beliefs.

In the next months the government made additional military, economic, and political concessions to German demands. It became increasingly clear to many people that Denmark was losing its political independence, something the Germans had promised to respect at the time of the invasion.

In November 1941 Danish Foreign Minister Erik Scavenius went to Berlin to sign the Anti-Comintern Pact. The pact, originally signed by the Axis powers of Germany, Italy, and Japan in 1936, united these countries in a battle against international communism and its leader, the

Danish Foreign Minister Erik Scavenius meeting with Adolf Hitler to sign the Anti-Comintern Pact

Soviet Union. In its conquest of Europe, Germany systematically forced the nations under its control to sign on. Now it was Denmark's turn.

～

Jørgen Kieler was not a communist. In fact, he considered himself anticommunist. But he was appalled at what was happening. Jørgen was a medical student, and in his circle of friends, the government's caving in to German demands was a constant topic of conversation.

Jørgen, like many other Danes, had sympathized with the Finns when the Soviet Union invaded their country in 1939. At the time, the Danish communists had been very unpopular because they supported the Soviet military action. But now everything had shifted. Instead of being political opponents, the communists had become martyrs, Jørgen thought, victims of an oppressive government policy.

It didn't matter that he disagreed with them, he told friends. These people had committed no crime, and yet they had been arrested. It was shameful.

When Foreign Minister Scavenius went to Berlin to sign the Anti-Comintern Pact, life at the university seemed to become one long, intense discussion. Everyone's fear was that by signing the pact, Denmark officially would be considered an ally of the Axis powers. This was "catastrophic," Jørgen and his colleagues believed.

When student friends planned a protest demonstration, Jørgen, his sisters, and his brother joined in. The organizers weren't communists. In fact, the demonstration only indirectly supported the communists. It was first and foremost a protest against the government "policy of negotiation."

It was supposed to be a peaceful demonstration, but the Danish police attacked the participants. The protest lasted for several days. Pictures and news reports of police beating and arresting fellow Danes shocked many people. For some, it was the beginning of active resistance that, until 1943, was directed against not only the German occupiers, but the Danish government as well.

At the demonstration on November 21, 1941, Jørgen Kieler was one of many students who were beaten. It was a day that changed his life.

The signing of the Anti-Comintern Pact sets off riots in Denmark.

Under the Nazi occupation, official news reports in Danish papers could not be completely trusted because of German censorship. The regular press was not allowed to write certain stories, especially if they were unfavorable to the Germans. At other times, newspapers were forced to publish the Nazi version of a story. And so Danes had to turn to other sources for information about events in Denmark as well as the world. Many listened to England's BBC radio broadcasts. Although illegal, it was easy to tune in.

Not long after the occupation began, illegal pamphlets started to appear. By the end of the first year, during the winter of 1940–1941, there were a few weekly underground newsletters. Information came from a variety of sources, from local observers to foreign broadcasts. The illegal press published more than just news. There were many jokes and satirical pieces directed at the Nazis.

Although as a whole Danes resented the invasion, most people

This illegal printing press was hidden in a dentist's office. (A photo reenactment done at the end of World War II.)

preferred some form of passive resistance—ridicule or other minor acts to make life a little more difficult or unpleasant for the Germans. Those involved in the underground press, however, wanted to encourage a more active resistance. They favored what they called "Norwegian conditions," for in Norway resistance groups actually fought against the Nazis. The pages of the underground papers reflected these concerns and included articles about appropriate targets for resistance and the pros and cons of sabotage.

In the beginning, the underground pamphlets were often single sheets of paper duplicated on copy machines hidden in attics and basements—any available, safe space. One paper, for example, was printed in a dental office, another, with great daring, in the sub-basement of Dagmarhus, the Nazi headquarters in Copenhagen.

Sometimes a small group of people would publish and print a paper for several months. Then, when discovered by the Nazis, the press would be closed down. Some editors when caught were imprisoned. Later in the war, others were tortured, some sent to concentration camps, and some killed. New people always took their place.

~

The morning the Germans invaded, Leib Beilin's mother fainted. She had lived in Denmark for thirty-three years, but the memory of pogroms in her native land of Russia was still vivid in her mind. Leib, whose friends called him Lui, was a Jew born in Denmark. He had never experienced such a fear, and his heart broke when he thought about his mother.

Lui, at age twenty-one, was the chairman of the Social Democratic party's youth group. He had been involved in the youth group since he was a teenager. Although the Social Democrats were officially against any form of resistance, Lui wasn't.

"Now we have to fight the Germans," he said to a small group of friends the day after the invasion. "The Danes as a whole may not want to, but I have to," he said. It turned out everyone in the group felt the same way. They all agreed the government was right not to fight the first day. "There are seventy-five million of them and only four and a half million of us," one friend said.

For several hours the group talked and talked, trying to figure out what they could do that would mean something. At last they decided to write a newsletter. They had a copy of the green leaflet the Germans had dropped. "The Germans are writing lies," Lui said. "We will give the people the truth." And so they wrote and printed several issues of a newspaper.

Then Lui became involved with another paper. He was responsible for all the material for one page. If a strike was organized, Lui covered it. When there were reports of sabotage actions, Lui wrote about them and any damage they caused. If the Germans claimed victory in battles in the Soviet Union or North Africa, and the BBC said otherwise, Lui corrected the news reports. He reported on anything and everything he saw and heard.

It saddened him, when he thought about it, that so few Jews were involved in the resistance, but personally he could not simply sit and wait. In whatever way he could, he had to fight. In fact, it gave him a particular pleasure to be Jewish and to be fighting the Nazis.

"We're very practical," he had explained to his mother. "I don't know who is working on what, or where. That way, if the Germans catch me, they won't get any information out of me, because I don't know anything." All Lui knew was that somewhere, some people had a mimeograph machine, and they printed copies of the paper that still other people distributed.

Lui's instructions were always simple. He was to go to a certain street corner with his typed page of material. He'd been told to look for someone wearing a certain-color shirt or jacket. He was to walk by the person and hand her or him an envelope with his page. No stopping, no talking.

~

In 1941 thirty-one illegal papers like Lui Beilin's were published. By the end of the war there were more than 530 such papers. Each of them reached increasing numbers of people. In the first year of the occupation some 1,200 copies were circulated, and during each year of the war the numbers increased dramatically. In 1944 nearly eleven million copies of illegal papers were printed. And still the numbers increased—in just the first four months of 1945, the last months of the war in Denmark, more than ten million copies were circulated.

Shortly after the arrests of communists in June 1941, members of the party who went underground began to publish *Land og Folk* (Land and People). It was a monthly paper that the Nazis were never able to shut down. By the end of the war more than five million copies had circulated throughout the country.

Then in a cooperative effort unique to Denmark, communists and conservatives joined together to publish another paper, *Frit Danmark* (Free Denmark). Political differences were set aside in the fight against a common enemy. *Frit Danmark* was first published as a monthly in April 1942. A year later, a weekly newsletter section of the paper appeared as well. By the end of the war more than six million copies of the paper had been printed.

Then, in 1943, a unique and illegal news service was established in Denmark. In fact, in all of occupied Europe, only Denmark had such a service. Founded by the reporter Børge Outze, it was called *Information.* The bulletin was published daily (except Sunday), and supplied stories and photographs for the underground papers to print.

Information was also smuggled out of the country to Sweden and to Britain. Copies were sometimes taped under German railroad cars crossing from Denmark to Sweden on boat trains. In the early years of the occupation, Danish businessmen sometimes hid copies that had been printed on extra-lightweight paper inside pens or pencils, which they took with them on trips across the Sound. Danish resistance fighters living in Sweden would then forward the bulletin to Britain.

Sabotage groups often sent *Information* reports of planned actions before they occurred. Photographers could then capture, for example, railroad tracks being blown up as the attack happened. The Germans desperately wanted to shut down *Information.* Four of Outze's close aides were caught and killed, but he eluded the Nazis by continually changing his headquarters. Finally, in October 1944, they caught him. Even then coworkers continued to publish the daily press bulletin.

During long hours of brutal questioning, Outze managed to convince the Nazis that he was disillusioned with the Allies and would now work for the Germans. When they released him, he immediately went back into hiding and continued to work on *Information* until the end of the war. In all, there were 473 daily *Information* bulletins from September 1943 until May 1945.

The illegal underground press, read by Danes throughout the country, served not only as a source of information, but also as a way of holding onto a sense of national identity in the face of the Nazi occupation. The very names, *Land og Folk* and *Frit Danmark*, were constant reminders that there was a common national goal whatever one's private political views were: free Denmark, its land and its people.

The Germans slowly began to lose patience with an occupation that was becoming less peaceful. One of the first organized sabotage groups was the Churchill Club. Its eleven members were teenage boys, ages fourteen to seventeen, who lived in the city of Aalborg in north Jutland. They stole weapons, set fire to railroad cars, put sugar into the gas tanks of German cars, and engaged in any other small sabotage actions they could think of. They were caught and arrested in the spring of 1942, tried, and convicted. Newspaper accounts quoted one of them as saying, "If you older folk will do nothing, we will have to do something instead."

Resistance was increasing on several different fronts. People organized themselves into groups, often around their work or other activ-

The teenagers known as the Churchill Club were one of Denmark's first organized sabotage groups. They were arrested in the spring of 1942.

ities. For example, there were resistance "rings" of doctors, nurses, ministers, architects, students, sports club members, teachers, and others. In one action, several hundred Danish doctors signed a petition that they presented to the government. The documents said the doctors would support the government if it would resist German attempts to impose rules in three areas. There must be

- no measures taken against Danish citizens that violated the Danish constitution
- no Danes drafted into the German army
- no measures, including deportation, imposed against Danish Jews

Dr. Karl Køster, a surgeon at Bispebjerg Hospital in Copenhagen, was one of the prime movers behind the petition, and later was an important resistance organizer in the events surrounding the Jews.

In early September 1942, in the face of increasing resistance activities, Danish Prime Minister Vilhelm Buhl, to appease the Germans, took to the airwaves and broadcast an appeal to Danes to refrain from acts of sabotage. He asked people to report any such acts to the police. Young people like Jørgen Kieler considered this attack on the resistance movement almost an act of treason by the prime minister. Kieler as well as others involved in the resistance felt that now their battle was as much against the Danish government as it was against the Germans.

Yet it was an act by the king himself that was the first serious threat to the government's policy of negotiation. On September 26, 1942, King Christian X celebrated his seventy-second birthday. Hitler sent the king a telegram effusive with greetings and congratulations. The king replied formally and tersely, "My utmost thanks. Christian Rex," triggering what has become known as the "telegram crisis."

Hitler, it was reported, flew into a rage. German diplomatic minister Renthe-Fink was ordered to deliver a protest to the Danish government. Hitler then removed Renthe-Fink from his job and recalled

Adolf Hitler named Dr. Werner Best the high commandant of Denmark in November 1942.

him to Germany. A month later, in early November 1942, Dr. Werner Best, the new high commandant of Denmark, arrived in Copenhagen. Best was a committed Nazi, and a member of the Gestapo and the dreaded SS. Hitler, it seemed, wanted to change the moderate Nazi policy in Denmark.

How would Best's arrival alter the occupation, and what would happen to the Jews? The state of occupation was a state of apprehension.

FIVE
RESISTANCE GROWS

IMMEDIATELY AFTER THE "TELEGRAM CRISIS" in late 1942, a weaker Danish government was finally formed, following weeks of negotiation with the new German high commandant, Dr. Best. With pressure from Best, Erik Scavenius, the unpopular foreign minister who had signed the Anti-Comintern Pact, became the new prime minister.

General Hermann von Hanneken had arrived to become commander-in-chief of the German military forces stationed in Denmark. Elsewhere, the Nazi war machine no longer seemed invincible. German troops were defeated at El Alamein in Egypt in November 1942, only to be driven completely out of North Africa the following spring. And on the Eastern front, the Germans were facing harsh winter conditions and a surprisingly fierce Soviet resistance to the German invasion. For the first time, Danes began to think that the Nazis might actually lose the war.

With pressure mounting, Germany had to protect its Western flank. General von Hanneken's main task was to prevent an allied invasion of Denmark. Fighting on several fronts, Germany more than ever needed Danish agricultural goods and industrial production to feed both the German people and their war machine.

Resistance, however, was increasing. Saboteurs attacked Danish factories and businesses that produced materials for Germany. Some resistance groups blew up railway lines to interfere with transports to Germany. All these actions interrupted the smooth running of the

German war effort, and General von Hanneken had orders to enforce tough measures against the resistance.

Late in 1942, encouraged, perhaps, by expectations of a new and harsher German command in the country, Danish Nazis tried again to burn down the Copenhagen synagogue. They managed to paint swastikas on the synagogue walls, but were prevented from firebombing the building by the Danish police. After the failed attack, the police formed a special auxiliary police unit of Danish Jews whose only task was to guard the synagogue. They also set up an electrical warning system between the synagogue and police headquarters.

The year 1943 actually began relatively calmly in Denmark. Werner Best, notwithstanding the fears upon his arrival in the country, continued the policies of his predecessor Renthe-Fink. He seemed to believe that in order to maintain the flow of goods to Germany from Denmark, the Germans had to refrain from antagonizing the Danes unnecessarily. In mid-January, Best sent a memorandum about the Jewish situation to Berlin. He reported that the Danish prime minister had said the whole government would resign if any actions were taken against the Jews.

Such restraint in attacks on Jews was unusual for the Nazis. At the Wannsee Conference in Berlin a year earlier, the Germans had discussed their plans for the "final solution," the extermination of all Europe's Jews. By that summer, the Nazis were forcing Jews in the occupied countries into concentration camps in the east. But not those from Denmark.

Rumors, however, of these transports had reached Denmark. In early 1943 the executive committee of the Jewish Community in Copenhagen met to discuss whether Denmark's Jews should prepare to flee the country. The committee concluded that it would be impossible to hide thousands of people without the help of non-Jewish Danes. The Viking Jews, who controlled the committee, did not think they could ask this of their neighbors. And so Jews in Denmark for the most part continued to sit and wait, with a few exceptions.

∾

Lui Beilin was in the civil service, made up of police, firefighters, and sanitation workers. He was one of the leaders of the fire brigade in his district. As a leader, he had a gold insignia on his uniform. With that insignia, he was free to walk the streets at night, even when the Germans imposed a curfew.

In fact, Lui had lots of freedom. As an official Danish government worker, he was responsible for handling certain German requests. When the Nazis took over a military barracks one time, they wanted new mattresses. Lui provided them.

But he was also part of the resistance. Sabotage actions were increasing, and Lui knew people who were involved in that. He handled their requests as well.

One day a man Lui didn't know came into his office. The man said the code words identifying him as a resistance fighter. After they talked for a while, the man said, "We're planning a sabotage action, an explosion. We need firemen's uniforms to wear as a disguise. Can you provide—"

"With pleasure," Lui interrupted.

For me as a Jew this is wonderful, he thought to himself. With this hand I give to the Germans, and with the other I strike at them.

~

As the war progressed, more people became involved in active resistance. If there was to be fighting in Denmark, the resistance needed weapons, but they were in short supply. And so some people made them themselves, others secretly brought them into Denmark from outside the country, and still others stole them.

~

Leif Vidø was a seventeen-year-old student when the Germans invaded Denmark. He felt angry and embarrassed at how easily Germany took over his country. And he remembered two years earlier, in 1938, when all the students had been called to a school assembly. It was right after British Prime Minister Neville Chamberlain had given in to Hitler's demands at their meeting in Munich. At the assembly, the headmaster had announced, "Chamberlain has brought peace in our time!"

Leif Vidø (on left) stole weapons from German soldiers and later, as a member of the Danish Brigade, participated in the liberation of Denmark.

Leif and his friends booed the headmaster that morning. Chamberlain had "sold" a part of Czechoslovakia to the Germans to secure peace, they believed. And what kind of peace could it be, when bought at the expense of the Czech people and the dismemberment of that country?

Now, two years later, Denmark was on the block. And the price was the very heart and soul of the country, its independence.

Leif and his friends wanted to do something. They hated seeing German soldiers nonchalantly walking the streets of Copenhagen. In the beginning they helped distribute copies of illegal newspapers. But they wanted to do more. Everybody was talking about getting arms. But how? Where? From whom?

Leif and three friends decided to go to La Tosca, a restaurant in Copenhagen that was popular with German soldiers. The soldiers would go there for dinner, and they'd usually drink a lot of schnapps. One of Leif's friends had noticed that when the soldiers hung up their jackets in the entranceway, they'd often hang up their gun belts as well.

The young men worked out a plan. They divided into pairs. Leif and one of the boys would do the "inside" work. As they neared the restaurant, both shivered slightly with excitement. Once inside, they looked around the dining room. They approached two soldiers who had several bottles of schnapps on the table, one already empty. They were eating and laughing loudly.

Leif, somewhat shyly, interrupted the soldiers' conversation. Eyes wide open in pretended innocence, he said, "We'd really like to know about the Wehrmacht. Could we ask you a few questions?"

The soldiers looked up and grinned broadly. One tipped back in his chair, almost falling over. He motioned to the boys to sit down. And for nearly an hour, Leif and his friend asked the soldiers questions. Enough questions to give their two other friends time in the lobby to sneak pistols out of the soldiers' holsters and get away.

∽

Some resistance groups were called "waiting groups." Their goal was to be heavily armed, trained, and ready to fight should the war physically come to Denmark. "Waiting" meant they had to be prepared. And of course they trained in secret. Groups in or near Copenhagen drilled several times a week in the Deer Park outside the center of the city, away from German patrols. Some held target practice in basements. But their biggest problem was the shortage of weapons.

∽

In 1942 Tage Seest learned to make guns. He had studied mechanical engineering at a technical university and was ready to put his training to use.

It all started when two friends came over one afternoon and said that the resistance needed weapons. They planned to start a workshop to make Sten guns. Tage knew about Sten guns. They were special 9-millimeter lightweight British machine guns. He joined the project.

First they had to find a place to set up equipment. The three stood looking at a small garage-like little building they had just rented. It was behind a main house. When they met with the owner, it was clear he was a Nazi sympathizer. They told him they were making scales and he promptly agreed on a rental fee. What could be more perfect, they thought, than a Danish Nazi housing a resistance cell!

There were metal parts lying all around the workshop and

scales in various stages of assembly. They hoped it looked convincing. Then the real work began.

They made mechanical drawings of a Sten gun, and Tage's friends copied pictures of the different parts he needed to assemble the whole gun. Then they took the separate parts drawings to metal shops around the city. They never told anyone what the part was for. They made up some explanation and simply asked if the factory could make 200 of this, or 75 of that.

One day the two returned with a carton of parts that Tage knew they didn't have the money to buy. They explained that they had gone to the Riffel Syndikat factory, a Danish company working for the Germans. They knew a rifle manufacturing company would have the parts.

One of Tage's friends had a machine gun under his coat. When they walked into the factory, he held up a sample, showed his gun, and told the factory manager they needed 200 parts. And they got them. Better the resistance take them than that they go to the Nazis!

It was much too dangerous to ask other factories to make the magazine for the ammunition. It was instantly recognizable as a gun part. So Tage made it himself. Then he assembled everything. He and his friends sold hundreds of the guns to the resistance. They charged only what it had cost them. This was not a profit-making business. This was war.

When the first hundred guns were completed, they decided to celebrate with lunch at the Bellavista Hotel. At the table they knew they didn't dare talk about guns, for who knew the politics of the waiter or the diners at nearby tables? You could never be too cautious. But it was a celebration, and they had to talk.

They raised their glasses to "one hundred perforating machines!"

❧

Weapons, whatever their source, had to be hidden, and that, too, was a part of resistance work. It was, in fact, a very dangerous activity. As the war progressed, the Germans became harsher in their punish-

Tage Seest demonstrates the "perforating machines" he and his friends made in their battle against the Nazis.

ments. Homes in which weapons were hidden were often blown up. And some resistance people who were caught with weapons were condemned to death.

〜

Bobs Peschcke-Køedt had just gotten a phone call with a cryptic message—"The sausages have arrived"—more weapons he was to pick up and distribute for hiding. Later in the day he told his group about the delivery. He wasn't sure what the load would be—pistols, submachine guns, rifles—it could be anything.

His brother Bibber was at the meeting. When everyone left, Bibber stayed on.

"Aunt Dux," Bobs said. "We can use her place."

Bibber smiled. "She's fantastic!"

At first Bobs had hesitated asking her, for the Germans had recently blown up several houses. But Bobs needed new hiding places. When he talked with Inger, she had agreed Aunt Dux should decide for herself what she wanted to do.

Aunt Dux was in her late sixties or early seventies, no one knew for sure, and she was a feisty lady at that. She lived in a house she had decorated inside with tiles and stained glass from Italy. It was colorful and beautiful, and as eccentric as Aunt Dux herself. She had a basement, where she was delighted to let Bobs and "his boys" hide their weapons.

Bobs had some rifles and machine guns buried in his own garden. He also had one gun in the house. It was an old, beautifully fashioned pistol that had belonged to the royal family at one time and somehow had come into his family's possession. He had it hidden in the cut-out center of a book.

Inger was in bed with the flu when a German officer telephoned. "Tell your husband to report to Dagmarhus this afternoon." Dagmarhus! Nazi headquarters in Copenhagen. Inger was terrified.

Someone must have reported that they had weapons, Bobs concluded when he heard the news. He decided to gamble and tell them about the antique pistol. Then he began to get ready. He took out his elegant suit. "You look just like the Prince of Wales," Inger laughed, as he put on his "plus fours." They were fancy knickers that came down almost to mid-calf. He wore them with patterned socks and dress shoes. Inger took the matching jacket off the hanger and handed it to him.

Then he left.

Inger knew Bobs could be a fast talker. That was her only hope.

Bobs Peschcke-Køedt in the same "plus fours" he wore to his Gestapo interrogation.

For the rest of the day she tossed feverishly in bed, unable to fall asleep.

When he arrived at Dagmarhus, Bobs demanded to see the top officer. "Of course I have a weapon," he announced boldly as he was ushered into an office. Bobs knew the Germans were cracking down on the resistance. He also knew the communists had been increasingly involved in sabotage actions. He himself wasn't a communist, but for the moment they were allies in the resistance. But pretending to attack them, he decided, was his best ploy.

"Do I look like a saboteur?" he demanded. "My God, you people know everything, so you must know I come from a wealthy family. With all these communist hooligans running around, of course I have a weapon. Here it is!" he announced proudly as he pulled the antique pistol out of a bag. "How else am I supposed to defend my family from these ruffians?"

The officer looked startled. Bobs talked on. At last, weary and almost apologetic, the officer said, "We have to confiscate it, but you can go now."

Clearly they don't know about the garden, Bobs thought, as he left.

After the war Anne and Bonnie would always say their father played the Scarlet Pimpernel with the Germans. "Check out the movie with Leslie Howard," they'd tell friends. "That was Pa!"

~

In March 1943, thinking to appease the Danes, Werner Best decided to permit elections to Parliament. Some resistance groups opposed any participation in the election, but most urged the population to vote. Five political parties issued a joint statement:

> The election of March 23 is different from all other elections. It does not concern the usual party differences. . . . The election should confirm the will of the people to defend that freedom which is our thousand-year legacy. . . . In this way, the election will be a confirmation of faith in Denmark and its future.

Nearly ninety percent of those eligible to vote went to the polls. Even Danes who had never bothered in past elections voted this time. It was a resounding victory for the government, and an equally resounding defeat for the Danish Nazi parties.

Although whipped at the polls, Danish Nazis continued to make their presence felt in Danish society.

~

Salli Besiakov lived in a large apartment complex in Amager, a part of Copenhagen about half an hour south of the city center. The complex was divided into two parts, each five stories high. Salli's building was on the sunny side. Across the field, the other building was always in the shade. Salli and his friends called that building "Sing Sing," after the American prison they'd heard about in the movies. It seemed especially grim to them, since many Danish Nazi families lived over there.

Salli's family lived on the first floor of his building. His parents had a tailor shop in a cellar work space just below, where they sewed mostly hats. Salli spent a lot of time in the workshop. His parents always sang while they worked. The window of the cellar shop looked across at Sing Sing.

Heintz and Fritz were "Sing Singers" around Salli's age. They were part of a Danish Nazi youth group, the Hitler *Jugend*, as they were called in German. They'd parade around the central open area in their black uniforms. Salli and his friends would sometimes fight with them. Salli's parents talked about the Nazis across the way, but for Salli, they were just Heintz and Fritz, "the bad guys." And no one was really afraid of them.

Sometimes Heintz and Fritz would cross the field between the buildings and scrape the window of the Besiakov shop, chanting nasty words about Jews. It took a while before Salli's parents resumed singing after one of these visits from Heintz and Fritz.

Mr. and Mrs. Besiakov had emigrated years before from Russia to Denmark. When the Russian revolution overthrew the tsar, life in Russia at first seemed to get better for Jews. And so Salli's parents, admiring the revolution from afar, became communists in Denmark.

Salli's mother learned Danish rather well. While her husband stayed in the shop, she would travel around the city to the different materials suppliers. Unlike most Jews, she was also active in the resistance. And unlike many communists, neither she nor her husband was arrested during the roundup in June 1941.

In the resistance, Mrs. Besiakov first helped with delivering underground papers. Then, since she knew who the Jews were, she visited all those she thought could contribute money. Jewish refugees who were socialists got help from the unions. Other Jews were aided by the Jewish Community's charity agency. Jews who were communists had nowhere to turn. These were the people Mrs. Besiakov helped.

In the spring of 1943, a regiment of Danish Nazis who had fought with the Germans on the Eastern front returned to Copenhagen. A large group of them gathered in Raadhuspladsen, one of the main public squares in Copenhagen. There was little sympathy for these Danes who wore the hateful Nazi uniform. An angry crowd surrounded them, and fights broke out.

Salli had ridden his bike into town that day. As he neared the square, he heard shouting. Curious, he rode into the square, but the crowd was so large, he couldn't see anything. The offices of the newspaper *Politiken* were across the way, and the second floor balcony faced the square. Salli left his bike in front of the building.

People were running out into the square as Salli made his way inside.

Hardly anyone was left in the building, and no one noticed him as he crossed the office floor to the balcony. He watched, fascinated as the Nazis were pressed into one corner of the square. A group of Hitler Jugend was with them. They all looked so strange—Danes in German uniforms.

He recognized two of the boys at the exact moment they saw him. Heintz and Fritz, and they were pointing at him! They tugged at a Nazi officer's sleeve. Salli was terrified they were saying. "Take him! Shoot him! Jew! Jew!" The crowd in the square pressed in on the Nazis, and the officer waved his gun in the air. Salli gripped the balcony rail, frozen for a brief moment. Then he bolted down the stairs, leapt on his bike, and pedaled so hard he felt dizzy.

He didn't stop pedaling until he arrived at his front door. When he caught his breath, he realized Heintz and Fritz weren't just "bad guys." They were Nazis. Suddenly the war was very close to home.

∼

Within five months of the March 1943 elections, the war against the Germans, for all intents and purposes, came to Denmark. No longer able to walk the fine line between acceding to German demands and maintaining a posture of independence, the government resigned. Denmark faced an uncertain future.

SIX
THE CRISIS LOOMS

DURING THE SUMMER of 1943, more than the weather heated up. In July it became a crime to annoy the Germans. One Dane was imprisoned for thirty days for speaking English to a German soldier. Another was sentenced to two years for sending an angry letter about Hitler and Germany to a local German officer. An elderly man was convicted and imprisoned for thirty days for insulting a group of passing German soldiers. Another received the same sentence for writing *Victoire* (victory, in French) on a German signboard.

Industrial sabotage, the bombing of factories and businesses doing work for the Germans, rose from 122 actions in 1942 to 969 in 1943. Attacks on railroad lines rose from 6 in 1942 to 175 the following year, and continued to increase until the end of the war.

A British organization called Special Operations Executive (SOE) had been established early in the war to coordinate resistance movements in German-occupied countries. Early attempts to parachute intelligence operatives into Denmark were unsuccessful. By 1943, however, contact was securely established, and secret radio communications were set up between Denmark and Britain. The British also launched bombing raids on Danish factories working for the Germans. When RAF planes crash-landed, or crews parachuted out, resistance groups tried to aid the downed officers. Whenever possible, they were taken to the coast and put on ships to Sweden, from where they made their way back to Britain.

Johan Legarth sat on the beach near Elsinore, waiting. Another pilot was coming tonight who had to be rowed to Sweden. It was good the sky was overcast. It still amazed Johan that he was a small part of a whole chain of help, and yet he knew so little of the whole story. Downed pilots were told to make their way to doctors or a local minister or priest. That much he knew. He also knew they'd be hidden at the Catholic cloister in Elsinore. Tonight another one was coming from the convent. But he didn't know if the man was English, Canadian, or American. Not that it mattered.

He watched the lights go out at the rubber factory. The night watchman was locking up the guard dogs. He could hear them barking. So far everything was on schedule. Someone had worked out this plan with the watchmen. He didn't know who, but again it didn't matter.

This was a four-person operation—Johan, a resistance friend, the pilot, and Johan's girlfriend. Actually, five, if you counted the night watchman. Once the dogs were locked in, the other resistance person would get a kayak that was stored in the basement of the factory and drag it to the water's edge. When the pilot arrived, they would paddle the few miles across the Sound to Sweden. Then Johan's colleague would return. Tonight Johan was the lookout. His girlfriend was his alibi should he need one.

There it was! He could see the shadow of the kayak by the water. The pilot emerged from the brush further up the shore. And Johan's girlfriend arrived. He checked his watch. Everything was

Johan Legarth worked for the resistance both in Denmark and later as a member of the Danish Brigade in Sweden.

exactly on time. He and his girlfriend would sit together in the lit-tle boathouse—just a couple out for the evening. But tonight they were more. They had to estimate the time of his friend's return, and in the pitch-blackness of the night, flash a light to show him where to land on the beach.

The Germans had patrol boats in the waters. It wasn't so bad when they moved, because you could just make out the low motor. When they decided to turn off the motor and float, that's when it was dangerous. Johan leaned back. It would be a long night.

~

Dozens of people were transported to Sweden in this fashion. Like all other forms of resistance, these acts in defiance of the Germans increased dramatically in 1943.

By August, incidents of sabotage had reached six or seven every day. German military equipment and installations as well as Danish businesses working for the Germans were all targets. The Germans were building a large warship in the city of Odense, a ship designed to set sea mines to prevent English submarines from entering the waters between Norway and Denmark. Saboteurs, in a daring and dangerous action, blew up the warship.

The wave of sabotage began in provincial towns like Esbjerg, Aalborg, and Aarhus. Finally it reached Copenhagen. The Germans reacted with force. Soldiers patrolled the streets, and the Schalburg Corps, a Danish Nazi SS force, was used to terrorize the populace.*

Enraged, Danes responded with strikes all across the nation. The mobilization and the imposition of curfews further incited the Danes. As the demonstrations turned violent, the Germans opened fire on crowds. The resistance movement had worked hard to arouse what they saw as the sleeping Danes. And Danes were now aroused.

Werner Best was recalled to Berlin. The day he left Copenhagen, members of Holger Danske, one of the major Danish sabotage groups, blew up the Forum building. The Forum was a large exhibi-tion hall that was being converted into barracks for German soldiers. Scheduled to open August 25, it lay in ruins on August 24.

---

*The Corps was named after the leader of a troop of Danish Nazi volunteers, the Frikorps (Free Corps), which had fought side by side with the Germans on the eastern front. Schalburg died in the east on June 2, 1942. Eight months later, a Danish SS force was named after him.

In August 1943 strikes break out throughout Denmark, unsettling the Germans and inspiring the Danes.

Best tried to convince Hitler and the other Nazi leaders that Danish sabotage was a passing phenomenon. It was still in Germany's best interests, he argued, to negotiate with the Danes, for more than ever Germany needed Danish agricultural production. Hitler was furious at events in Denmark. He refused to see Best and instead issued his orders through Joachim von Ribbentrop, his foreign minister. Best returned to Denmark with instructions to hand the Danish government an ultimatum the Germans knew would never be accepted. Martial law would then be imposed, and the Nazi crackdown could begin.

On August 28, 1943, Best presented the Danish government with the ultimatum. There were to be no public gatherings of more than five people, and no strikes. An 8:30 P.M. curfew would be strictly enforced, and direct censorship of the press imposed. Harshest of all, the Germans declared that attacks on German soldiers, possession of firearms or explosives, and acts of sabotage would be immediately punishable by death.

The Danish government's response was an unequivocal "No." The government finally abandoned the "policy of negotiation" that had so provoked resistance activists. During the night of August 28, German soldiers swept through Copenhagen, taking over government buildings and services. The royal palace was surrounded, leaving the king a virtual prisoner for the duration of the emergency. The government submitted its resignation, although civil service ministers continued to perform administrative functions. No new government was formed.

When they turned on their radios the morning of August 29, Danes heard German General von Hanneken declare,

> Recent events have shown that the Danish government is no longer able to maintain peace and order in Denmark. The disturbances provoked by hostile agents are aimed directly at the Wehrmacht. Therefore . . . I declare a military state of emergency in the whole of Denmark.

Among other regulations, he announced that provoking or encouraging a strike harmful to German interests was an act punishable by death.

With lightning speed, German soldiers arrested dozens of prominent citizens, including the top officers of the armed forces. The rear admiral of the navy managed to signal his ships, "Scuttle or escape to Sweden!" This order defying the Nazis was successful: twenty-nine ships were scuttled, thirteen made their way to Sweden, and only six were taken by the Germans. Denmark was under martial law.

Børge and Dora Thing had been living in a small apartment in Copenhagen with their infant daughter Jette. They were communists, but had avoided arrest in the roundup of June 1941. Then, in late 1942, Børge and a few friends set fire to several factories working for the Germans, and Børge went partially underground. He continued to go to work, but he never slept at home. Instead, he stayed with different people, always rotating, always on the move. Dora and little Jette returned to live with Dora's parents.

In the early months of 1943, Børge's sabotage group blew up a Danish aluminum factory that produced materials for the Nazis. After that, Børge went "a hundred percent" underground—no work, no public meetings. The Danish police, working with the Germans, searched for him. They had no clear evidence of his sabotage activities, but they knew he was a communist.

Dora would get messages to be at a specific street corner at a certain time on a particular day. She and Børge would spend an hour together, never knowing when they'd meet again.

April 18 was Børge's birthday. Ever since he and Dora had met, they had always spent their birthdays together. He convinced himself the police would never pick that day to come after him. He couldn't have been more wrong. When he arrived at his in-laws' apartment, the police were waiting. He was arrested, convicted under the new law banning communist organizations, and given an eight months' sentence. Had they known of his sabotage activities, he would most likely have been sentenced to death.

For nearly four months Dora frantically awaited news. Was he being tortured? Was he still alive? Then word came that he'd been taken from prison to the hospital with severe headaches.

All morning on August 29, Dora listened to radio reports about the state of emergency. By mid-afternoon she decided to do a little shopping. As she waited for a light to change, a woman took her arm. She whispered softly but urgently, "Take street clothes to Børge. He's waiting." Then she vanished into the crowd.

Dora Recht Thing helped her saboteur husband, Børge, to escape.

Dora packed a shopping bag with Børge's clothes. A suitcase might suggest travel, but a shopping bag would look ordinary. When she arrived at the hospital, she and Børge talked about everyday things. If anyone was listening, they sounded like an average couple—a concerned wife visiting her sick husband. Børge quickly dressed. He whispered he'd see her soon, but he didn't know exactly when.

As she left the hospital, Dora noticed a car waiting by a side door. She crossed the street to a newsstand, bought a paper, and watched. Within minutes Børge emerged and walked quickly to the car.

It was a week before Dora got a message telling her to be at a specific street corner, at a certain time . . .

Børge Thing had escaped on the very day dozens of other people were arrested. Over the next year he was so active and successful a saboteur, he became the head of BOPA ("Borgerlige Partisanar" or "Civil Partisans"), one of the two main organized resistance groups.

~

Before the August state of emergency, in the spring of 1943, Jørgen Kieler was printing the underground paper *Frit Danmark* in his apartment in Copenhagen. He didn't write or edit the paper. He was involved only in printing and distribution, but he was becoming dissatisfied. He disagreed with some of the paper's political positions and had decided to leave.

To Jørgen, every factory that was burned or blown up was another strike, however small, for a free Denmark. He had been delighted when the paper came out in support of sabotage. But now they were saying only factory workers, not students, should be involved in such actions. "The workers would know what to blow up . . . they'd have the contacts . . ."—these were the arguments the paper used. Students like Jørgen, on the other hand, should work on the illegal press. But sabotage was a crime punishable by death. Working for the underground press was not. It was wrong, he thought, to say factory workers could risk their lives, but not students.

Besides, students had early on understood the importance of resisting the Germans. They'd been in the fight from the beginning.

They should be allowed to be part of any action against the Wehrmacht. Sabotage was also an important way to tell the despised prime minister, Scavenius, and the Danish government to stop collaborating with the Nazis. Jørgen wanted to send that message. And so he left the paper.

But how do you become involved in sabotage? It's not as if you can look up "Sabotage" in the phone book and find a group. Tensions had been rising all summer. People were very hesitant to talk about illegal activities. The person you were chatting with might be a spy. In an atmosphere of such general wariness, Jørgen couldn't simply start asking around. He knew that the two main saboteur groups were BOPA, which was largely communist, and Holger Danske. But he also knew that you have to know someone who knows someone who knows. . . . And Jørgen didn't.

He returned to his home in Jutland to work for the summer at the local hospital. He looked up his old friend Peer Borup. They managed to collect a few weapons and two small bombs. Excited to be really "doing something," they planned their first sabotage action. They knew nothing about explosives, nothing about pistols, nothing about the techniques of sabotage. And they had no one to teach them. But with a brashness made up of innocence and arrogance, they decided to blow up a railroad bridge on a Saturday night. They picked August 28, 1943.

It was pouring when the two reached the bridge that night. They didn't know where to put the bombs. They stood for a few minutes, trapped in their ignorance and getting wetter by the minute. Then they walked out onto the bridge and strapped the bombs down. After they set the timers, they returned to their homes.

Jørgen knew that the head of the hospital's X-ray department was very sympathetic toward the resistance. And so he had enlisted the doctor's help earlier in the week. The night of August 28, the doctor was to be at a dinner party with a colleague who lived near the bridge. When they all heard an explosion, the doctor was to call the police and report a bombing.

Timing was crucial, for Jørgen and Peer had learned that a large factory nearby was also going to be blown up that same night. If the police rushed to the bridge, they wouldn't be able to interfere with the factory sabotage.

The sound of the explosion stopped the dinner table conversation, and Jørgen's doctor friend urged his host to telephone the police. The report was called in, just as Jørgen had planned.

Peer and Jørgen met early the next morning. They couldn't wait to check out the damage their bombs had caused. One was an incendiary bomb, the kind that would start a fire. But the bridge, they realized too late, was made of iron, so there was nothing to burn. Surely, though, there would be some damage from the other bomb. When they reached the bridge, it was still standing. In fact, they could see nothing at all amiss. They walked across slowly and carefully. There, in the middle where they had placed the explosive bomb, was a small hole in a metal plate.

They turned back and walked home in silence. It was clear they had a lot to learn.

At least the factory was destroyed, they comforted themselves. And they both felt a little better. They decided to collect more explosives. Jørgen would return to Copenhagen, and Peer would stay in Jutland to search for supplies.

Jørgen left immediately for the capital. As far as he knew nothing had changed except the fact that he was now a saboteur—not an entirely successful one but, nonetheless, a saboteur. At his apartment, his sisters and brother greeted him with the news of martial law.

The next day, travel into and out of Copenhagen was cut off. Although he didn't yet know it, Jørgen was about to begin another phase of his resistance work.

∼

The state of emergency declared on August 29, 1943, lasted until October 6. The Germans now set about arresting prominent Danes, some of whom were Jews.

∼

BAM! BAM! BAM! A fierce banging on the front door awakened Leo and his brother. It sounded like a rifle butt, Leo thought, as he tried to see his brother in the darkness of the bedroom they shared. He got up and crossed the room. The pounding in his chest was almost as loud as the pounding on the front door.

Leo's father blocked the doorway of the bedroom. "It's the Germans!" he whispered hoarsely.

"We have to open," Leo said. "Otherwise they'll break down the door."

"No!" his father said. As chief cantor of the synagogue, Mr. Goldberger had a commanding presence. Leo admired him enormously and rarely challenged him. This time he had to.

"But it'll only be worse if they break in," he pleaded. His father shook his head resolutely. If they started to break in, he'd hide, he said. Hide? Leo thought. That was inconceivable. His father under the bed? Behind clothes in the closet? It made no sense. Leo's mother and two younger brothers were at the summer house they rented on the coast. Had she been home, she'd have made his father understand.

BAM! BAM! The pounding became more insistent.

"IT'S THREE O'CLOCK IN THE MORNING! STOP THAT RACKET!" It was their upstairs neighbor yelling. Leo's father made a silencing motion with his finger across his lips.

"IF YOU DON'T STOP, I'LL CALL THE POLICE!" Like most Danes, their neighbor resented the occupation. It was bad enough to have to put up with Germans all over the place, but to be awakened at three in the morning, well, that was too much.

"WHERE ARE THE GOLDBERGERS?" one of the Germans yelled. So that was it. They've come for us at last, Leo thought. They didn't know their neighbor particularly well. Leo had seen him that afternoon, so the man knew at least some of the Goldbergers were home. He felt a sudden chill. Would the neighbor give them away? His father gripped Leo's shoulder. With his other hand he continued to motion silence.

"THEY'RE IN THE COUNTRY," the neighbor shouted. "GO AWAY!"

Leo, his brother, and his father stood like people carved in stone. Minutes stretched out unbearably. At last a motor started up in the street, and they heard a car pull away. Leo peered out cautiously from behind the window shade. A truck remained parked outside the building. Two soldiers leaned against it. Guards, Leo groaned inwardly. We're trapped in here.

Mr. Goldberger led the way down the staircase off the kitchen into the air-raid shelter in the basement. The three of them sat in silence. Leo watched in amazement as his father propped a small mirror on a shelf and began to shave off the trim beard that so immediately identified him.

When he finished, Mr. Goldberger decided to send his sons outside to see what was happening. And most important, to check if the trains were running. The plan was to flee Copenhagen and go to their summerhouse in Rungsted that very night.

Leo and his brother crossed through an inner courtyard and were able to exit onto another street away from the waiting truck.

Nothing! they reported when they returned. No tanks, no soldiers, and the Nørreport station was open.

Less than twenty-four hours after the Germans had banged on their door, Leo and his father and brother were on a train headed north. As they pulled into the Rungsted station, Mr. Goldberger told the boys to go to the summerhouse without him. He would stay in different places in case the Germans searched for him up here. He'd be in touch, he told them. And then he left.

The next day the Goldbergers learned the country was under martial law, and that a state of emergency had been declared. Within days they also heard that Rabbi Friediger, chief rabbi of the Copenhagen synagogue, had been arrested along with other prominent people.

For nearly two weeks, Cantor Goldberger remained in hiding, always checking in with his wife by telephone. From news accounts, it appeared at last that tensions had eased somewhat. The Jewish High Holidays of Rosh Hashanah and Yom Kippur were approaching, and Cantor Goldberger felt he had to return to the city. They'd had a narrow escape, but for how long, no one knew.

SEVEN

WARNING

WHEN THE DANISH GOVERNMENT and king rejected the German ultimatum, Denmark turned a corner. Hitler removed Best from his post as high commandant and placed General von Hanneken in charge. Best was now to report to the general. Tensions between the two remained for the duration of the war.

Although no longer the top German officer in the country, Best still exercised considerable authority. On the day martial law was imposed, he called a meeting of Danish newspaper editors. "In this ridiculous little country," he railed, "the press has inoculated the people with the idea that Germany is weak. . . . You have received [our answer] during the night." He concluded with a threat: "Each editor will be responsible with his head for seeing that the people are no longer poisoned.[5]" At that time, both the number and circulation of underground newspapers were increasing dramatically.

Pressure on the Jewish community was beginning. Just days after the declaration of martial law, membership lists were confiscated from the office of the attorney for the Jewish Community. When the Jewish leadership reported the incident to a Danish official, Nils Svenningsen, director of the foreign ministry, he immediately complained to Werner Best. Best denied any knowledge of the event. A week later Best sent a telegram to his superiors in Berlin:

IN ACCORDANCE WITH THE CONSISTENT APPLICATION OF THE NEW POLICY IN DENMARK, IT IS MY OPINION THAT MEASURES

SHOULD NOW BE TAKEN TOWARD A SOLU-
TION OF THE PROBLEM...OF THE JEWS...

Best argued in his telegram that the action against the Jews should take place while the state of emergency was still in effect, for he believed that the roundup would provoke a general strike and the cessation of all cooperation from Danish governmental bodies. And so he concluded:

IN ORDER TO ARREST AND DEPORT [ALL THE] JEWS AT ONE SWEEP IT IS NECESSARY TO HAVE THE POLICE FORCES I REQUESTED . . .[6]

During Best's August recall to Berlin, Hitler had reportedly said that the freedom of the Danish Jews was "loathsome" to him. Pleased at Best's new tough approach, Hitler now reappointed him as high commandant. Once again General von Hanneken reported to Best. A week after Best's telegram, Hitler wired his formal approval of a plan to deport the Danish Jews.

The crisis was moving inexorably closer. Rumors based on little information but much fear rapidly circulated among the Jews. The close ties between the Jewish leadership and Director Svenningsen calmed some people, but not all.

Early in the morning of September 17, German soldiers entered the Copenhagen synagogue and seized the Community's librarian from a prayer service. They took him back to the Community Center offices where they conducted a full-scale search for membership lists. When Svenningsen complained about this latest raid to Best, Best admitted knowing about it. It was, however, only a "small action," he said, a routine search for saboteurs having nothing to do with the Jewish question. Best expanded on the lie, repeatedly assuring Svenningsen there were no plans for actions against the Jews.

Svenningsen reported this to the Jewish leaders, some of whom believed it, or at least wanted to. Nonetheless, news of the raid and fear that it was the beginning of a roundup swept through the Jewish community. A few people managed to leave for Sweden, but most waited for the leadership to act. The leaders were predominantly Viking Jews, and surely, the community thought, they had the contacts, the funds, the sophistication to know what to do. But the community waited in vain, for their leaders simply refused to believe this could happen in Denmark.

The Nazis, however, did not wait. Gestapo agents and additional German SS troops arrived in Denmark, with men from Adolf Eichmann's office of Jewish affairs. Eichmann was in charge of carrying out the "Final Solution," the plan to kill all of Europe's Jews. Denmark's Jews were to be next. To aid in the roundup, two Nazi police battalions arrived in Copenhagen in the last two weeks of September.

The top German officials in Denmark knew their attack on the Danish Jews would be extremely unpopular. As the date of the action neared, telegrams and memoranda went back and forth between Denmark and Berlin. Although Werner Best and General von Hanneken were political rivals for control of Denmark, each for his own reasons sought to stop, or at least postpone, the raid. These Nazi leaders, it was very clear, were not interested in protecting the Jews. Rather, they wanted to protect Germany's relationship with Denmark, for they were still dependent on Danish production. General von Hanneken tried to persuade his superiors in Berlin that the prestige of the army in Denmark would be seriously harmed if the planned roundup was carried out. The response from Berlin was a heavy line drawn through the memorandum, "Nonsense" written in the margin. With Hitler supporting the deportation of the Danish Jews, there was no stopping the action.

Rumors of a planned action were so rampant, Fuglsang-Damgaard, the bishop of Copenhagen, questioned Best, who absolutely denied any such plans. In fact, in all his talks with the Danes, Best repeatedly stated there was no planned action against the Jews. With these very strong statements from the German high commandant, Director Svenningsen and the bishop once again reassured the Jewish leaders that their community was safe.

At the very time Best was denying any planned attack, two German ships were en route to Copenhagen, scheduled to arrive on September 29. In what the Germans planned as a "lightning attack" on the night of October 1 and 2, all of Denmark's Jews were to be rounded up and transported to the Theresienstadt concentration camp in Czechoslovakia.

∾

Georg F. Duckwitz was a German who had lived in Denmark for fifteen years. When the occupation began, he became head of German shipping operations, and worked closely with Werner Best. When Best told him of the plans to round up the Jews, Duckwitz argued with him, saying it was a terrible mistake.

Over the years he had lived in Denmark, Duckwitz had developed a longstanding relationship with certain leaders of the Social Democratic party. For some of those years, he had also been a German military intelligence agent, a spy of sorts. But by 1943, some of the Danish politicians were not merely contacts, but also friends.

In mid-September when Best had told him what was planned,

On September 28, 1943, Georg F. Duckwitz, a German, warns the Social Democrats of the planned roundup of Denmark's Jews.

Duckwitz had written in his diary, "I know what I have to do." On September 28, when he learned the date of the planned raid, he acted.

Duckwitz knew the Social Democrats were meeting at the Workers' Assembly House on Roemer Street. When he entered the meeting room, he pulled aside Hans Hedtoft, head of the party. Duckwitz was pale, and his voice shook as he said, "The disaster is here! Everything is planned in detail." He told Hedtoft that in less than twenty-four hours ships would anchor in Copenhagen's harbor for the transport of the Jews "to an unknown fate."

Hedtoft was stunned. "Thank you for telling me," was all he blurted out. Duckwitz turned quickly and left. Hedtoft and other party leaders, H. C. Hansen, former Prime Minister Buhl, and Alsing Andersen, knew that the Jews had to be warned. They divided up assignments.

Hedtoft left to inform C. B. Henriques, president of the Jewish Community. When he arrived, Hedtoft asked to see Henriques in private.

"Mr. Henriques," he said as soon as the door was closed, "a terrible disaster is about to happen. The action against the Jews is imminent. You must warn every single Jew in this town immediately."

Henriques stared at him in disbelief. "You're lying!" he said. "This can't be true . . . Director Svenningsen has just assured me earlier today . . . No, I don't believe it!"

It took all of Hedtoft's powers of persuasion to convince Henriques. Obviously, he said, the Germans had been lying to Svenningsen, as to all of them. This latest information was from the highest of sources. And with that, Hedtoft left.[7]

∽

On Tuesday, September 28, 1943, Lui Beilin sat in his office in Søborg, just outside of Copenhagen. As a fire brigade leader, he had been trying to clear the paperwork off his desk all afternoon. Memos, letters, lists, and more memos—he sometimes thought it was endless. Lui looked up. A man he didn't know stood in the doorway. The man gave him a message to go immediately to H. C. Hansen's office.

H. C. Hansen was a friend. Through all the years Lui had been involved with the Social Democratic Party youth, he'd gotten to know H. C. well. What could be so important? Lui wondered. It was dangerous to use the telephone, so Lui left the office and rode his bike to Copenhagen.

It was a clear, crisp day, the kind Lui normally delighted in. Today, he was preoccupied. At the Social Democratic Party head-quarters, he was taken into a side room by Hansen's secretary.

"Lui," she urged him, "you have to tell all the Jewish people you know to go into hiding. From tonight on they cannot stay in their homes!"

Lui went straight to his parents' house. His mother had just returned home herself and was hanging up her coat. She put it back on even before Lui finished speaking. The two left the house together and went off in different directions to spread the news. Lui turned to look at his mother as she walked hurriedly down the street. She had, after all, been right to fear a pogrom, even here, he thought to himself sadly. Then he brushed the thought aside. There wasn't time to be sad. He went to spread the news.

~

Alsing Andersen, one of the Social Democratic Party leaders, related the startling information from Duckwitz to his secretary, Inge Barfeldt. She was married to a German Jewish refugee, who had been training to become a farmer-settler in Palestine. When she couldn't reach her hus-band, she called Julius Margolinsky, one of the organizers of the halutz-im trainees. It was near curfew time, but Inge went to Margolinsky's home. News of this nature couldn't wait.

Margolinsky acted immediately. He sent Inge to Rabbi Marcus Melchior, who was functioning as chief rabbi since Rabbi Friediger's arrest during the August 29 raids. Then he set up a system to contact all the halutzim training centers.

The leaders of the Jewish community had so depended on infor-mation that originated with Werner Best, they were totally unprepared for the truth that broke over them like a sudden thunderstorm. Unlike

Mr. Henriques, however, Mr. Margolinsky and Rabbi Melchior under-stood the significance of the news immediately. Margolinsky's warning system for the agricultural trainees was the only real organizational planning by any Jewish leader.

For Rabbi Melchior, after the raids on the Community Center files and the imposition of martial law, the pattern was clear. October 1, the night of the planned raid, was a Friday night, the beginning of the Jewish Sabbath and also the second day of Rosh Hashanah, the Jewish New Year. The Germans had planned cleverly, the rabbi thought, in assuming that most Jews would be home that evening.

Rabbi Melchior knew there wasn't much time. The fastest way to reach many Jews, he reasoned, would be to say something at services the next morning.

~

Leo Goldberger was annoyed. He didn't want to go to morning services. But a cantor's son, his father said, had to set a good exam-ple. Leo wasn't interested in setting a good example. He was inter-ested in staying in bed for at least another half hour. Besides, he knew he was "insurance"—they needed at least ten men, a minyan, in order to hold services. He had turned thirteen in June and had been bar mitzvahed, so he could help make up that minyan.

"I'm not getting paid for this," he grumbled as he dressed.

He walked down the synagogue aisle with his father. As he looked around, he guessed there were probably eighty people in the synagogue that morning. They hadn't needed him for a minyan after all. When he took his seat, he noticed the rabbi wasn't wearing his usual robe. That's odd, he thought to himself. Leo then joined in the singing his father led and forgot about the rabbi's outfit.

Suddenly, Rabbi Melchior stood up and went over to the can-tor and whispered to him. He held up his hands and stopped the service. Leo strained forward. Could he be hearing right? A roundup? No services this morning? Everyone had to go into hid-ing immediately?

Leo looked at his father. They had just come out of hiding.

The Copenhagen synagogue, the setting for Rabbi Melchior's announcement that all Jews had to go into hiding immediately

When the Germans had banged on their door in the middle of the night just a month ago, Leo had been more frightened than ever before in his entire life. Now, it seemed it was all happening again.

∽

News of the planned raid swept through Copenhagen. Friends told other friends who told relatives who told still other friends, both Jewish and Christian. People who had not been involved in the resistance joined in to warn anyone they could think of, even people they did not know. Everyone had to work fast.

The story of Jørgen Knudsen, a young ambulance driver, is typical of the spontaneous outpouring of help.[8] On his way to work on the morning of September 29, Knudsen saw some friends stopping people in the streets. When he learned what was happening, he rushed to a telephone booth, tore out the phone book, and went to the garage to pick up his ambulance. He didn't go to work that morning. Instead, he marked any names in the book that he thought were Jewish. Then he drove to their homes to warn them of the impending raid. If someone didn't have a place to hide, he took them to Bispebjerg Hospital where he worked. Knudsen knew that Dr. Karl Køster, who had organized the doctors' protest petition the year before, would help.

The planned action against their countrymen appalled most Danes. On September 30, before the actual roundup began, the leader of all the Danish economic groups (including employers' associations, trade unions, industrial and agricultural boards, shipowners, chambers of commerce) sent a protest letter to Werner Best:

> In the event of such an action taking place, it will in our view, to a great extent harm the efforts being made from our side to create peace and order in Denmark. The Jews here in Denmark form a part of the country's population and a step against them will affect the whole Danish people.

The king sent a protest letter as well, informing Best that "special measures against a group of people who have enjoyed full civic rights in Denmark for more than one hundred years could have the most severe consequences."

The roundup took place on October 1 and 2. After ten o'clock at night, telephone lines in Copenhagen were shut down. German soldiers were under orders not to break down doors, for top German officials were still trying to maintain the fiction of a relatively peaceful occupation. The Danish Nazis accompanying the German soldiers did not always feel such compunctions, however. Sometimes doorbells were rung, and if there was no answer, the Germans moved on. Other times raiding parties broke in and conducted searches. But few Jews were to be found. The warnings had largely succeeded, for on this issue, as none other, Danes were united. Denmark's Jews, eluding the Nazis' grasp, were in hiding.

EIGHT
ESCAPE

THE RAID WAS A STUNNING FAILURE, since nearly ninety-five percent of the Jews had evaded the roundup. Nonetheless, Werner Best tried to make the action appear successful. He reported to Berlin that Denmark was *Judenrein* (clean of Jews). The truth was, the Jews were in hiding, preparing to flee the country. It was clear German officials in Denmark were as quick to lie to Berlin as to the Danes.

The difference was, the Danes had caught on. Many Danish soldiers had been arrested when martial law was declared on August 29. The Danes had been arguing for their release ever since. The day after the October raid against the Jews, the Germans announced:

> As a result of measures taken by the German authorities, the Jews have been removed from public life and prevented from continuing to poison the atmosphere, for it is they who have to a considerable degree been responsible for the deterioration of the situation in Denmark through anti-German incitement and moral and material support for acts of terror and sabotage. In the next few days...release of the interned Danish soldiers will begin.

Danes were enraged by the announcement. So many were involved in helping to hide Jews, they scorned the lie immediately. Even more infuriating to them, the Germans were trying to turn the Jews into scapegoats, the cause of all Denmark's problems. The imprisoned Danish military commanders refused to be released under such conditions. They would not be a part of any attack on Danish

Jews. Neither would most other Danes. As one historian described it, it was as if "a living wall raised by the Danish people in one night" protected their countrymen.[9]

Thousands of Danes hid their fellow countrymen. Denmark is, however, a small, flat country in which it is not easy to hide people for long, particularly when both German and Danish Nazis are searching for them. In order to help, Danes opened their pocketbooks, their houses, and their hearts. With the Nazi crackdown, many Jews without any contacts had fled to the woods surrounding Copenhagen. Danish student search parties found them and engineered their escape. Others were hidden in private homes and empty summerhouses. People huddled in warehouses, stables, barns, hotels, cellars, and church lofts—anywhere Danes could think to hide them.

∾

Inger Peschcke-Køedt stood in the kitchen washing dishes. She was exhausted. That night a young Jewish boy and his mother were staying in the cellar room. When her husband Bobs had said he was helping Jews to escape, she had thought, Of course they must be helped. When he said he wanted to hide people in their basement room, she had paused before she answered. She wasn't afraid for

Inger Peschcke-Køedt was a young mother, but that didn't stop her from hiding Jews in her basement. Anne, left; Bonnie, right

herself or Bobs. But Anne and Bonnie were so little, she wanted to keep them from any possible danger. It was only a moment's hesitation, though. Yes, of course, they must do this.

The mother and son had sat at the dinner table, their eyes darting back and forth at the slightest noise. But it was the boy's hands that startled Inger. They trembled, sometimes more, sometimes less, but all the time.

Then the boy told them a story. He had studied in Germany before the war had started. He hadn't told anyone he was Jewish. He was simply a Dane. His German teachers had looked at his light hair and tall stance, and pronounced him a "perfect Aryan." When he finished the story, they had all laughed at the absurdity of the Nazis, and then grown quiet.

Two days later Inger was reading in the living room when the telephone rang. She heard Bobs answer it. "Yes, yes, of course come over."

It was Jens needing a place to stay, Bobs explained. Inger was relieved it was a friend, not someone they had to hide. She fixed up the cellar room and then went to bed. She was too tired to wait up for Jens.

She was awakened by a banging on the front door. She heard Bobs's voice rising in irritation. Several men were talking all at once. She could hear their footsteps coming closer to the bedroom. The door opened, and she pulled the quilt tightly around her.

"They think we're hiding Jews," Bobs said, his voice heavy with sarcasm. "They're searching."

They were Danish Nazis, and she hated them even more than the Germans. They went through the house, opening closets and shoving aside clothing. They even searched the closet in the children's bedroom. At least they didn't wake them, she thought angrily.

Inger heard them going down to the basement. They'd see Jens's things down there, nothing else. Finally, they left. Only then did she get out of bed. In the living room, Bobs and Jens were laughing. Apparently these Nazis had been listening in on their telephone line and knew someone was staying overnight. "Did they really think we'd be so stupid as to talk on the phone about hiding people?" Bobs asked.

Bobs and Jens told Inger that the best part was when the Nazis had first come in. They had demanded to know if someone was staying over. Jens sauntered out of the kitchen. "Yes, of course. I am." One glance at his pale blond hair and his identification papers and the Nazis accepted the fact that he wasn't Jewish. But they searched anyway.

"Well," said Bobs, "now we know for sure that they're tapping the phone."

"And now we know two examples of a 'perfect Aryan'—one Jewish and one not," Inger murmured.

Then she left the two in the living room and went back to bed. She wondered who might be the next person to stay in their cellar room. Tonight they had been lucky. The Nazis had come two days late. She crept under the quilt and stared at the shade-covered window.

~

Salli Besiakov's parents had been arguing for days. They had heard of the planned raid from friends. When Mrs. Besiakov had picked up the illegal papers to distribute, that was all people talked about. Salli's father had first dismissed the news as groundless rumor. His mother had argued that since they couldn't know for sure, they had to prepare.

"They've even announced it in the synagogue," Mrs. Besiakov said. Salli's parents never went to the synagogue. In fact, they were always disagreeing about politics with their religious relatives. This information seemed to wipe out any remaining resistance from his father. If even the religious ones were preparing, surely, then, he would have to.

Salli helped his mother get the suitcases out of the closet. There was very little to pack, and so the three of them sat in the living room and waited until dark. Salli had never seen his mother so distracted yet so determined. It confused him, and he sat quietly.

"Now!" she said suddenly. It was dark as they made their way

Salli Besiakov with his parents,
shortly before their escape to Sweden.

carefully across the open field. Salli still found it hard to believe they were actually going over to Sing Sing, the building across the way. "We can't go there. They're all Nazis over there!" he had shouted earlier.

There was an exhausted look on his mother's face. "There are good people everywhere, even in Sing Sing," she'd said. In fact, Salli learned, most people in Sing Sing were not Nazis.

"What about Heintz and Fritz?" he persisted. "And all their friends?" "Yes," she repeated, "they're there." Then she'd had no more time to talk. And now they were headed over to Sing Sing.

They climbed the stairs to the third floor and knocked softly on the door of the Bjørners' apartment. They had passed no one, and Salli's parents seemed relieved. Nothing was said until they were in the apartment with the door locked behind them.

"I can't thank you enough," Salli's mother said, shaking Mr. Bjørner's hand. He just smiled and welcomed them all into his home.

It took a long time for Salli to fall asleep that night. He tossed, it seemed, for hours on the couch. Too many thoughts were clattering around in his head. Would he ever go back to his home? How long would they stay here? What about his friends? If he went out, would he bump into Heintz and Fritz?

He was awakened by the sound of car motors. In the dark he made out the shadow of his father and mother at the living room window. He made his way over to them.

One of the German "prairie wagons" was parked in front of his building across the way. Salli had heard about these trucks with their canvas tops. German soldiers filled them with Danes who'd never be seen again. That's what some of the kids had said. When he asked his mother about it, she had simply nodded.

Salli leaned forward, pressing against the window. That flashlight inside an apartment over there—it was in *his* apartment! *The Germans were searching his apartment!* Salli shivered and moved closer to his parents.

~

Miriam Ruben understood that they had to leave their apartment that very minute. "The Germans are coming! You can't stay!" the landlady kept repeating.

Miriam was five years old, but she knew a lot. She knew, for example, that some Germans had an apartment in the building. She had been told not to talk to them. The landlady was saying something about "Jews." Her mother made a quick phone call and then ran for their coats.

Mrs. Ruben took Miriam's hand and they rushed down the back staircase. Miriam could hear the German boots stomping down the hallway on the landing above them. Then she and her mother were out on the street, and she couldn't hear the Germans anymore.

"Where's Papa?" she asked, as they walked quickly away from the building.

"He's waiting for us," her mother answered.

Miriam's father was at the train station when they arrived. The trip up the coast to Vedbaek took about half an hour. Miriam hadn't been there before.

"This, unfortunately, is the safest place," the woman said.

Miriam stared at the horse stables. What did the lady mean by "safest place"?

Miriam's mother leaned down and said quietly, "We're staying here tonight."

"Sleeping in the stable?"

Her mother nodded. Miriam was glad she was wearing her warm coat.

⁓

The immediate and obvious goal in the escape effort was to get the Jews across the Sound to safety in Sweden. The distance between Denmark and Sweden varies along the coastline of Zealand, the largest of the Danish islands, from two to fifteen miles. Distance, however, was not the main problem. Fishermen faced imprisonment and forfeiture of their boats if they were caught taking people to Sweden. They also had to weave their way through minefields the Germans had laid in the Sound. Although the mines were designed to blow up metal boats and most of the fishing vessels were wooden, they sometimes still caused damage.

Before October, Sweden, as a neutral country, had done much to aid the German war machine, but the tide was turning. Hitler had suffered defeats in North Africa and the Soviet Union. In the fall of 1943, it looked as if Germany might lose the war after all.

Then, world-renowned nuclear physicist Niels Bohr fled Denmark. Bohr was part Jewish and crossed the Sound September 30, when news of the planned roundup had been confirmed. The allies wanted Bohr to fly immediately to London from Sweden. But Bohr insisted on speaking to the Swedish foreign minister and then the Swedish king, asking them to provide a safe haven for Denmark's Jews.

The Swedish government had, at the request of others, earlier notified Berlin that it was prepared to take in all the Danish Jews. Having been turned down by the German high command, however, Sweden had dropped the plan. But the evening after the king's meeting with Bohr, Swedish radio broadcast the news that Sweden would accept all Jews from Denmark. Only then did Bohr fly to England.

"Money and boats," Jørgen said. "That's what we need." When Jørgen Kieler returned to Copenhagen August 29, he had planned to collect explosives, learn whatever he could about setting them, and then return to Jutland to continue sabotage actions with his friend Peer. Instead, trapped in town by the state of emergency, he jumped right back into the political discussions he had been a part of before he left.

With news of the planned roundup of the Jews, all the talk abruptly stopped. Now there was only one concern, and that was how to save the Jews.

Money and boats. Jørgen's sister Elsebet and a friend set out one Friday afternoon to visit rich estate owners outside of Copenhagen. Sunday evening when they arrived back at the apartment, they had collected thousands of kroner.

Ebba Lund and her sister were in Jørgen's group. Jørgen knew they spent their summer vacations on the island of Christians Ø, where many of the fishermen were their friends. Perhaps they could find someone with a boat in Copenhagen.

Ebba had heard of a fisherman in the city, called the "American." He had lived for a while in the United States and was known as an odd fellow, but with a lot of friends. She found him living in a little fishing hut in Nordhavn, the northern part of the harbor of Copenhagen.

Ebba Lund and her friends secretly organized a fleet of twelve boats to transport Jews to Sweden.

She asked him if he would be willing to take some Jews across to Sweden. The American was squatting by his fishing nets. She added he would be well paid. He agreed to help.

The group now had a boat. The next day Ebba asked the American if he knew other fishermen who'd be interested. Within a short time, Ebba, Jørgen, and the others had organized a fleet of nearly a dozen boats.

The group now had money and boats, but, they realized, no Jews. As if responding to a call, Jørgen's sabotage partner, Peer, suddenly appeared at the apartment with a Jewish couple who were refugees from Czechoslovakia. They had been in Jutland and had contacted Jørgen's father. Peer brought them across the country to Copenhagen.

Ebba took them to the American. After they were safely on board, she told the group that the couple had been fleeing the Nazis from one country to another, and now once again they were leaving a Nazi-occupied land, this time, however, for a neutral, safe country. They were the first of hundreds that Jørgen, Ebba, and the rest of their group helped to freedom.

∽

On the night of the German raids, Bent Bogratschew's family split up. His mother, older sister, and little brother stayed with a neighbor in their apartment building in Copenhagen. Bent and his father went to the home of a friend. Later his mother told him that she could hear the Germans pounding on their apartment door. When no one answered, the soldiers left.

Bent's father and uncle had emigrated to Denmark from Russia as teenagers. After years of hard work, they now owned their own tailor shop. They arranged to turn over the business to a Swedish employee who was not only a trusted worker, but also a good friend. If and when they returned to Denmark, the man agreed to transfer the business back to them.

After the first night in hiding, the family reunited and stayed at the Swedish employee's home for the rest of the week. He arranged for a fishing boat to take them to Sweden the night of October 7.

Bent's grandmother was to come with them. Before they left for the pier, Mrs. Bogratschew put medicine drops into a small cube of sugar and gave it to the baby to suck. He fell asleep immediately.

There were ten people on the boat that night, six in Bent's family, and four strangers. The four were "Viking Jews," whose ancestors had lived in Denmark for hundreds of years.

The boat was to take them to the Swedish island of Ven. It was a stone-fishing boat, Bent's father explained to him. From the bottom of the Sound, the crew gathered big stones that would be used to build piers. The boat's crew continued to work, slowly moving through the water, so that it would look like a normal trip to any boats patrolling the area. Down in the hold, the passengers hid in the darkness.

After some hours at sea, the medication wore off, and Bent's little brother woke up and began to cry. The man from the other family cut through the noise and said sharply, "Throw him overboard!"

Mrs. Bogratschew remained calm. She scarcely looked at the man. In a quiet voice she explained she would give her son some medication and he would fall asleep in no time. She spoke patiently to this grown man as if he were a child who had just said something very stupid. Bent looked at his little brother, peacefully falling asleep in his mother's arms. The little boy of course hadn't known what the man had said. But Bent—he would never forget those words.

Suddenly the door to the hold was pulled open, and several Danish policemen stared down at them. "Not so many," one of them said. "Have a good trip!" Words Bent also would never forget. With that, the door was bolted down. There was a stunned silence. Then the grown-ups began whispering.

The boat continued to fish the waters for stones. Normally, it is a twenty-minute trip from Copenhagen to Ven. This time, the trip took twenty-four hours.

～

The seaport town of Gilleleje was one of the main embarkation ports for Sweden. It is estimated that nearly one fifth of the Jews who fled

Gilleleje harbor, departure point for about one fifth of all Jews who fled Denmark in October 1943

Denmark in October 1943 passed through Gilleleje. The town, with a population of about 1,700, was too small for people to hide their rescue efforts. They counted on their neighbors not to betray them. In fact, so many residents were involved, a rescue committee formed to coordinate all the activities—finding housing for the refugees and scheduling boat departures. Dozens of Jews on any given day or night might be hidden in Gilleleje and then transported to Sweden. It was as if the town itself had become an actor in the rescue.

~

The first night on the run, Leif Wassermann, his mother, and his sister were hidden in a hospital ward. His father stayed with non-Jewish friends. The next day Mr. Wassermann arranged for a car to take the family to their summerhouse in Rungsted. They drove on back roads to avoid German patrol cars. Leif knew they were running away, but at age five, he wasn't exactly sure what they were running from.

The third day the Wassermann family, including Leif's grandparents, went farther up the coast to Gilleleje. Leif's uncle was married to a woman who wasn't Jewish. They had a house in Gilleleje, and she and her friends were helping people to escape.

That night Leif and his family crouched on the floor of a house about two miles from the harbor. Outside, German soldiers were scouring the building and grounds with their flashlights. Leif watched shafts of light streak across the floor from the crack under the front door. He could hear the Germans talking and their dogs barking. Leif's grandmother started to cough. His father quickly put his hands over her mouth and pressed tightly. Leif was sure everyone could hear the muffled sounds.

At last the patrol was gone. Leif's aunt came to check on them. Throughout the night she went back and forth to the harbor. Not yet, she'd say.

At about four o'clock in the morning, she announced it was time. A car waited outside to take them to the harbor. Leif, his mother, sister, and grandparents climbed into the car. There was no room left for his father. No matter, Mr. Wassermann said. He'd walk.

Leif didn't understand how his father would find his way. The night was truly black. No moon, no stars to give a little light. Later, his father told him that all along the road people stood in doorways telling him where to go. It was an act of kindness Leif would never forget.

～

A well-known coordination point for escape to the coastal ports was a bookstore in downtown Copenhagen across from Nazi headquarters in Dagmarhus. If a copy of a book of poems by Kaj Munk, the celebrated poet, playwright, and theologian, was in the window, it was safe for Jews to come into the store. The owner, Mogens Staffeldt, and friends then organized transportation to the fishing boats and escorted people in their flight. Staffeldt took a singular pleasure in defying the Nazis right under their very noses.

∾

Ebba Lund and Jørgen Kieler also worked their rescue operations from the center of Copenhagen, and always during the day, never at night.

It was the safest time, Ebba argued. Who would think anyone would defy the Germans in broad daylight?

Ebba's code name was "Little Red Riding Hood." It was easy for people to remember. They were told to find the lady in the red hat, and she would help them.

Actually, Ebba was the end of the line. Jørgen and Flemming Kieler and another friend were the guards at the entrance to the harbor, and they had pistols. At least three times German patrols had come by and then disappeared when they saw the armed guards. Sometimes the Germans simply didn't want to start a fight. Other times, they had been bribed.

After those fleeing had passed the armed patrol, they were taken by the Kieler sisters and other members of the group down to the harbor, where they were turned over to Little Red Riding Hood who put them on the boats. Most of those fleeing the country were Jews, but this chain of rescue also helped people from the resistance who were being hunted and deserters from the German army.

Although some Danish police and German patrols turned their backs and didn't interfere, there were others that did arrest people who helped the runaways. Kieler and Lund's group had been lucky. So far nobody had been stopped.

Late one afternoon after Ebba had put several passengers on a boat, a German patrol came walking out onto the pier, headed in her direction. Ebba had already taken off her red hat and shoved it into her handbag. But she still had about 10,000 kroner in the bag. If the Germans found that…she didn't know what would happen.

A few fishermen looked up from their work and watched the patrol approach. Ebba made a quick decision. She walked up to one of the fishermen. She took his arm and smiled romantically at him. Pretend with me, she silently urged him. He smiled back at her. The Germans stared for a moment at this "young couple," and then turned away.

In a few short weeks in October 1943, Ebba and Jørgen's group helped some 700 to 800 Jews flee Denmark.

~

The story of the fishing town of Dragør, about half an hour south of the center of Copenhagen, is often overlooked in histories of the rescue. About 2,100 people lived in Dragør in 1943, and almost everyone in the town knew about the rescue efforts. Indeed, most townspeople were involved. Some 600 or 700 Jews, most at the beginning of October, sailed to Sweden on Dragør fishing boats. Initially, the German commandant stationed in Dragør seems to have looked the other way, for it is unlikely he did not know what everyone else in Dragør knew—that hundreds of people were fleeing to Sweden from the town's harbor.

On October 4, 1943, however, Nazi officials, alerted, it is believed, by an informant, cracked down. It was a cold, wet, and windy Monday night. At eight P.M., a bus with Wehrmacht soldiers suddenly appeared at the harbor. Tragically, several taxis filled with Jews arrived at exactly the same time. The German soldiers began shooting. No one was killed, but more than a dozen Jews were arrested, imprisoned, and later shipped to Theresienstadt concentration camp. Others fled into the darkness and hiding.

That same night, a Danish boat not involved in rescue activities struck a German mine in the sound not far from Dragør. Ambulances rushed to the scene to help the injured sailors. Dr. Poul Dich, a local doctor, transformed the rescue of the seamen into a Jewish rescue operation as well. He hid Jews disguised as patients in the ambulances, alongside the sailors. Late that night and early the next day the ambulances with their lights flashing and sirens screaming raced to hospitals in Copenhagen. The Jewish "patients" were then sent to other ports to flee to Sweden.

Dr. Dich was not unusual, for doctors and nurses throughout Denmark helped in the rescue operations. In particular, Bispebjerg Hospital in Copenhagen played an extraordinary role, hiding Jewish "patients" in hospital wards and nurses' quarters. Some two thousand or more people passed through that hospital on their way to Sweden and freedom. Other hospitals were also involved in rescue operations.

∼

At first Dora Thing wasn't sure she should flee. Although she was Jewish, she was married to a Gentile. But when they thought about their thirteen-month-old daughter Jette, Dora and her husband, Børge, decided it was safer for her to go to Sweden. The Nazis had failed in the initial roundup, but they were still searching for Jews. Børge would stay in hiding in Copenhagen. He had escaped from the Nazis once and now wanted to continue his sabotage activities.

Børge arranged everything. He found a fisherman willing to take them and paid in advance for passage for Dora, Jette, and Dora's eighteen-year-old brother Leopold. Benjamin, Leopold's best friend, would join them.

They were to meet the fisherman at midnight on the beach at Espergaerde, about forty minutes north of Copenhagen. In the late afternoon of the day of flight, they took a train up the coast. Dora met with a doctor before they went to the beach.

It won't hurt much, the doctor promised her. It would only put Jette to sleep. The sound of a baby's crying, Dora knew, could easily alert a German patrol boat. The doctor then gave Jette an injection.

The hours passed slowly as they huddled in the brush near the pier. An old man with his son and a teenage brother and sister also waited. So there are eight of us, Dora thought. She wondered how big the boat was.

When the fisherman emerged from the shadows, they started toward him, then stopped. A stranger had appeared on the beach. Was this a trap? Dora's arms tightened around the sleeping Jette.

They watched as the stranger reached into her bag and handed the fisherman a wad of money. He pocketed it and led her and several people who had followed her onto his boat. Dora's group ran toward him.

"You have our money! We are supposed to be on your boat!" Dora insisted.

The fisherman shrugged. "She gave more," he said. He went to board the boat, when almost as an afterthought he turned back and said, "Of course, I do have a rowboat. You can have it for an additional payment."

Row to Sweden! Dora was stunned. The old man sighed, as if he knew escape was now impossible. The brother and sister looked at each other, and Leopold and Benjamin stared at Dora. "Yes, of course, we'll take it," she said.

Moments later they were alone on the beach. They dragged the rowboat into the water and climbed in one at a time. The young girl held Jette while Dora stepped into the rocking boat. It had been a long day, and Dora was glad to let the girl hold Jette for a little while longer.

As they moved slowly away from the shore, Dora realized that the rowboat was leaking. Water in the bottom of the boat almost reached her ankles. While Leopold and Benjamin rowed, the old man and his son used their hats to try to bail the water out. But the level kept rising. Denmark receded into the darkness.

When they were nearly a quarter of a mile offshore, the water was near the top of the boat. The old man suddenly lost his balance and fell overboard. He tried to keep his head above the black, swirling water, but his heavy winter coat pulled him down. His son leapt in after him. One moment, there were two people in the water, coughing, sputtering, arms flailing. The next moment, nothing.

"They're gone!" Dora cried. The young girl was still holding Jette. Until this moment, she had sat immobile, the water rising around her. Now swept by a nameless terror, she let out a harsh cry, stood up, and threw Jette into the water.

In the next instant, Leopold dove over the side to catch Jette who, like a small package, was sinking to the bottom. He surfaced with her in his arms. Dora moaned as she reached for the still child. Was she alive or dead? She held the limp body close to her and began to sob.

No one knew how far they had drifted. The Danish coast was dark and beyond sight. The lights of Sweden seemed close. Leopold stripped off his coat and said he was sure he could make it to Sweden. The young girl jumped in after him, and the two swam toward the lights.

Benjamin and the girl's brother treaded water, one on each side of the boat, trying to keep it from tipping. Dora stood holding the baby and crying into the night.

At least an hour passed. At last a boat appeared through the mist. A Danish fishing boat! Dora sank down, dizzy with relief. But when they were all on board, the boat owner refused to sail to Sweden. Instead, he threatened to turn them over to the Germans. When Dora opened her mouth to protest, not a sound came out. It was as if all her strength of mind and body had been washed away in the churning water. Then, a small miracle! The ship's crew took control of the boat and forced the owner to sail back to Elsinore. Back in Denmark the waterlogged four were taken to the local hospital.

When Dora woke up the next morning, she cried out, "My daughter! Where's Jette, my daughter?" She struggled to get out of bed. The nurse wheeled Dora's bed into the adjoining room.

Jette was bouncing on Leopold's lap, her head thrown back, laughing with an infant's total abandon.

Leopold Recht holding Jette Thing, whom he rescued from drowning during their harrowing escape attempt.

Leopold and the teenage girl, exhausted from a much longer swim than they had anticipated, had been washed back up on the Danish shore near Elsinore. Fishermen had brought them to the same hospital.

German soldiers made routine hospital checks. Although medical records were altered and names changed to avoid detection, it was safest to leave a hospital as soon as possible. In a few days, the small group was taken to the home of a dentist, active in the rescue actions, who lived nearby.

Jette arrived wrapped in a hospital gown and blankets. Her clothes had been ruined and discarded. The next morning the dentist's daughter shyly offered Dora some baby's clothing. It was a gift from her doll, she explained.

Several days later, six people, one dressed in doll's clothing, made their way safely across the Sound to Sweden, where they remained until the war was over.

∽

The fact that some fishermen charged exorbitant fees, or that some Germans accepted bribes or looked the other way during the rescue operation, in no way diminishes the feat of the vast majority of the fishermen. And although the rescue was largely successful, there were later reprisals. After the failure of the Nazi raid, a number of German officials were replaced by more hard-line Gestapo officers. Although most fishermen were not caught during the escapes, many, including some from Dragør, were arrested over the following months. Some were imprisoned and tortured, and others were sent to concentration camps.

Danish clergy also played an important role in the rescue operation. Some ninety percent of all ministers took part in the rescue and resistance efforts. On Sunday, October 3, a little over a day after the failure of the Nazi roundup, Lutheran ministers read a letter from pulpits across the country. Bishop Fuglsang-Damgaard had sent the letter to the German officials and to every Danish Lutheran minister. He wrote that the Lord Jesus Christ was born a Jew. He continued:

Persecution of the Jews conflicts with…the message which Christ's church set out to preach. Christ taught us that every man has a value in the eyes of God.…Whenever Jews are persecuted because of their religion or race, it is the duty of the Christian Church to protest…, because it is in conflict with the sense of justice inherent in the Danish people and inseparable from our Danish Christian culture through centuries… Notwithstanding our separate religious beliefs, we will fight to preserve for our Jewish brothers and sisters the same freedom we ourselves value more than life.[10]

That same day, the sacred Torah scrolls were secretly removed from the main synagogue in Copenhagen and hidden in a church nearby. Also on that day, Adolf Eichmann arrived in Denmark to check on the continuing search for Jews. For the first time in the Nazis' brief but brutal reign in Europe, Jews in large numbers had escaped their grasp. Fifteen years after the war, awaiting trial in Israel, Eichmann wrote a two-part memoir published in *Life* magazine. In describing transports of Jews from different European countries to concentration camps, he complained that Denmark "posed the greatest difficulties of all," for most of the Jews had escaped.[11]

Train ticket to coast for escape to Sweden. (Note: Roundtrip fare purchased to deceive pursuing police and Nazis.)

NINE
CAPTURE

NOVELS AND HISTORIES ABOUT DENMARK during the war focus on the extraordinary rescue of the Danish Jews. But not all of Denmark's Jews escaped. Nearly 500 were captured and sent to Theresienstadt concentration camp. A number of them had gotten no warning; others, believing such a roundup could not happen in Denmark, had ignored it. Some were betrayed by *stikkers* (informers). Still others were too weak or exhausted to flee. A small number of Jews died while trying to escape. Others, unwilling to risk falling into the hands of the Nazis, took their own lives. Their stories are also a part of Denmark's history.

During the early hours of the raid, the Nazis seized the residents of the Jewish old-age home next to the Copenhagen synagogue. At first, a small group of soldiers arrived on foot. Some minutes later, seven large trucks arrived with additional soldiers and attack dogs. One elderly resident committed suicide. Twenty-nine others were arrested. The attack on the home was singularly violent:

> [A]ll the inmates, aged from sixty to ninety, were taken away. The Germans behaved here with incredible brutality. They burst into the room of an old lady who was paralyzed and had been bedridden for eleven years, and since she could not get up they bound her with leather straps and dragged her to the synagogue, where all the old people were assembled. Here they were cross-examined as to their acquaintance with this or that saboteur and since it was only natural that they did not know any, they were beaten and

kicked. From the synagogue, as from all the rooms, the Germans stole any valuables they could lay their hands on; and the German police troops relieved themselves in the synagogue.[12]

Werner Best refused to see Director Svenningsen until near midnight on October 1, as the raid was happening. Best then acknowledged for the first time that the Hitler regime considered the Jews in Denmark to be enemies of the Reich. All those arrested, he informed Svenningsen, would be transported to Czechoslovakia. Only half-Jews and those married to non-Jews would be spared.

~

Birgit Krasnik's father was a tailor who sang in the synagogue choir every Saturday morning. He was not, however, in the synagogue on the Wednesday morning Rabbi Melchior warned the congregation about the impending raid.

When he first heard the news, he thought, I didn't do anything. I make clothes and I'm not politically involved, so they won't take us. But within days, realizing the seriousness of the danger, he and several friends went to find a fisherman to take them to Sweden. They were betrayed, and Isaac Krasnik and his friends were arrested and thrown into the Copenhagen jail.

Rachel Leah Krasnik, Birgit's mother, was afraid. Where was Isaac? Why hadn't he come home? She went to her parents. Isaac had been ill with tuberculosis and had spent many months in a hospital. Perhaps he had had another attack, her father suggested. Why not check with the police?

At the local police station, the officer on duty found nothing in the records about Mr. Krasnik. He suggested she ask at German headquarters in Dagmarhus in downtown Copenhagen. Although Mrs. Krasnik had heard the rumors about a mass arrest of Jews, her fear for her husband overrode all other thoughts.

"Oh, yes, Mrs. Krasnik," the Nazi officer at the front desk said quite pleasantly. "Your husband will be here this evening. Come, and bring your daughter." She didn't think to question how he knew she had a daughter. This was the morning of October 1.

Mrs. Krasnik's mother-in-law had planned to go into Dagmarhus with them, but at the front door of the building she suddenly changed her mind. "I'd better go home, or I'll be late making dinner. We can talk tomorrow." She gave Birgit and her daughter-in-law a hug and hurried off.

When Birgit and Mrs. Krasnik walked into Nazi headquarters, they were taken to a dark room and told to wait. Birgit began to cry. Soon her whimpers turned into sobs and then screams, "Where is my father? He's not here! Where is he?" Nothing seemed to calm her. At last an officer took them up to the first floor and left them in another room.

Mrs. Krasnik looked around her and recognized several friends. And like Mrs. Krasnik, too many had followed the instructions. With a sinking voice, she said to Birgit, "Now you must be quiet. This is awful, what I have done." The words pierced through Birgit's tears.

Mrs. Krasnik knew her parents were preparing the Rosh Hashanah dinner. She also knew with an absolute certainty they'd be arrested if she didn't warn them. But how could she? It was a miracle, she thought, that Isaac's mother had not walked into Dagmarhus with them.

Birgit and her mother sat for hours. Late in the evening they heard footsteps on the staircase. The door was thrust open and German soldiers came in with their guns pointed at the little group waiting inside. *"Schnell! Schnell!"* ("Hurry up!") they ordered. The group ran, half stumbling down the stairs. In the street they were forced into waiting police cars, the kind used to transport criminals. Birgit clung to her mother's hand. The cars drove to the harbor where German transport ships waited.

A bitter wind whipped around the group as it stood on the dock surrounded by soldiers with their rifles cocked. Birgit shivered. At five, she was one of the youngest in the group. Someone was handing her a hat. She looked up. A young girl, perhaps ten years old, smiled down at her. "Thank you!" Birgit cried, as she put it on. It was blue with a red design, and she felt instantly warmer.

At last they were told to board the ship, and they all climbed

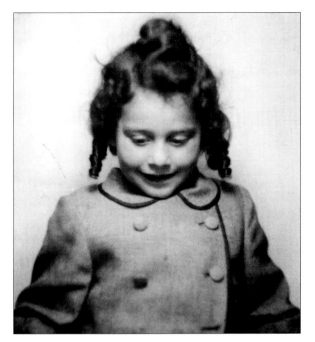

Birgit Krasnik, shortly before her capture, in the coat she wore to Theresienstadt

down to a lower deck. Some people stood, some squatted down. Birgit lay on the floor, exhausted, and fell asleep.

When she opened her eyes, her father was standing in the doorway. She rushed over and buried her face in his coat. He looked awful, she thought. The Gestapo had pressed him, he said, for names and addresses of Jewish friends. When he refused to talk, they had beaten him. But that was all over now, he said softly, brushing Birgit's hair away from her face. Now they were together. The three Krasniks stood with their arms around each other.

A short while later, Mrs. Krasnik's parents came down the steps. With them were her brother and two sisters. Later she learned that another brother and sister had escaped to Sweden.

Birgit fell asleep again, this time to the grinding of the motor as the ship pulled out of the harbor into the darkness. When she awakened, she was on her way to Theresienstadt.

Johan Legarth had just had his tonsils out, and his throat hurt. All he wanted was to crawl into bed and try to sleep. But there was no time. He had gotten a message to go to a veterinarian's office.

When Johan arrived, there were some thirty or thirty-five peo- ple standing in small groups. They looked frightened and agitated. A few were quietly crying.

Johan's throat ached. He wondered if he had a slight fever. But as the doctor explained the situation to him, he forgot his discom- fort. These people were going to be picked up and taken north to the town of Gilleleje and then to Sweden. A truck would arrive for them within one hour. Two hours at most, the doctor assured him. Could Johan help to calm them down?

So Johan took off his coat and introduced himself to the group. He thought his voice sounded strange, but then nobody there knew him. Many times he had helped people to Sweden, he told them. British pilots, resistance people on the run—they all went across the Sound. It was not a bad trip, he told them. Not bad at all. He had also worked with fishermen. They were good in these waters, he assured them.

The room was filled with people of all ages. Johan smiled, turn- ing from one to the next. He had one job, and one job only—to cheer them up. He began at six o'clock. By seven o'clock, some in the room seemed more relaxed. At eight o'clock, Johan was still talking, telling stories of the different rescues he had been a part of or knew about. By nine o'clock, others were also telling stories. At ten o'clock, although definitely calmer, people began to wonder aloud when the truck would arrive. At eleven o'clock, it finally did. It was a canvas- covered truck, and everyone piled in. As the truck pulled away, the doctor told Johan they were headed for the church in Gilleleje.

~

On the evening of October 5, the Gestapo swept into Gilleleje just as boats were about to sail for Sweden. Ten or fifteen Jews were caught. Hundreds fled back into hiding, and the Gestapo left town. But the Germans returned to Gilleleje the next night. In a surprise raid on the Gilleleje church, some eighty Jews were trapped and caught. A few were released because they were half-Jews. One of those hiding in the church the night of the raid recalled a room full of frightened people. The Germans shoved them down the stairs, yelling at them as if they were animals. Outside the church, they were forced to walk between two lines of German soldiers pointing bayonets at them. Then they were put on trucks and sent to Theresienstadt.[13]

It is now believed that a woman, not from Gilleleje, was the *stikker* who betrayed them. She worked at a hotel that was a hiding place for many Jews. Her boyfriend, it is said, was a German soldier who had been sent to the Russian front. She thought if she helped the Gestapo, perhaps he would be brought back to Denmark. Her boyfriend was not brought back, but her betrayal sent the largest group of Jews caught in Denmark at one time to a Nazi concentration camp. The people Johan Legarth had spent nearly five hours with were among those caught in the Gilleleje church arrests.

∾

The loft of the Gilleleje church, where some eighty Jews were betrayed and captured by the Germans

It was a long summer, Salo Wassermann thought. He was eighteen and ready to go back to the city. Usually in mid-August the family left their summerhouse in Espergaerde and returned to Copenhagen. But this summer was different. There were strikes all over the country. And then the Germans had declared martial law and a state of emergency on August 29. It was hard to know what was going to happen. Salo's parents decided to stay in the summerhouse for a little while longer.

Salo's father was a tailor with a shop in Copenhagen. He had come from Poland when he was sixteen years old. Salo's mother had come from Russia as an infant. The family had had the summerhouse in Espergaerde for nearly a dozen years, and Salo's mother knew just about everyone in the village.

In October, the family still hadn't returned to Copenhagen. Mrs. Wassermann knew her mother had been captured at the old-age home. Now she wanted to protect the rest of her family. Early one morning at the harbor, Mrs. Wassermann learned from an old fisherman that many Jews were coming to town, asking to be taken to Sweden.

Mrs. Wassermann said she, too, wanted to make those arrangements. "But you're not Jewish," the fisherman said, somewhat startled.

"Of course I am," she replied. Until that moment, it had never been of interest to anyone what her religion was. Now, it was all-important.

At first the Wassermanns decided that since they were so well known in Espergaerde, perhaps it would be better if they left from another town. They went to stay with a friend further up the coast. As soon as they arrived, however, they realized it was a grave mistake. Hitler Jugend lived next door. To be that close to the Nazis was just too dangerous.

And so the Wassermanns returned to their summerhouse and made other arrangements. They would leave from Snekkersten, a nearby town, on October 4. Shortly before they were to go, Mr. Wassermann surprised the family. "I can't go tonight," he said. He was obviously unhappy about the decision, but he had made up his mind. "I have worked my whole life. I can't just let the shop go. I must go back to Copenhagen to make arrangements. I will come over tomorrow."

Salo's father had already left for Copenhagen when the contact arrived to tell the family it was time to go. Mrs. Wassermann wanted to wait for her husband's return. This was not possible, the contact said. They must leave immediately.

Late that afternoon Salo, his mother, sister, brother, and nine other relatives hid in a home atop a hill looking down on the Snekkersten harbor. It was dark when they began to climb down the little path to the beach. Suddenly someone shouted, "GO BACK! GO BACK! THE GERMANS ARE COMING!" Within minutes another voice shouted, "NOW! COME NOW AND HURRY! HURRY!"

Down on the dock, Salo was the last to jump on the fishing boat. It pulled away immediately. As he looked around, he could see all of his relatives—aunts, uncles, and cousins. And there were three strangers, a young couple with a child. Salo thought about his father. He knew he'd see him in a day or two.

As the boat moved out of hearing range, Salo stared at the Danish shoreline and watched a remarkable event in pantomime. The doctor who had given medication to the young children to keep them quiet was parking his car diagonally across the pier, preventing several rapidly approaching German cars from reaching the end of the dock. Soldiers were waving their arms and pistols, but the doctor seemed not to be paying attention. He wasn't about to let the Germans catch these people he had just helped.

Salo's boat moved steadily toward the lights of Sweden. Within an hour, they arrived, and the fishing boat turned back to Denmark.

Later that night, the crews of eight fishing boats that had left from Snekkersten were arrested on their return, and that escape route was closed down.

Mr. Wassermann returned the next day to their summerhouse and found a fisherman with a rowboat willing to make the trip. That evening eleven people piled into the small boat—Mr. Wassermann

Salo Wasserman, center, and his brother and sister shortly after their arrival in Sweden

and six of his relatives, two fishermen from the village, and two people Mr. Wassermann did not know.

For several days in Helsingborg, Sweden, Salo and his mother asked about the boat they thought Mr. Wassermann had sailed on. They were told there was no information about such a boat or such a person.

Then one day when they asked, they learned that the boat had capsized and nine of the eleven people had drowned. One of them was Salo's father. Mr. Wassermann was forty-six years old when he died fleeing the Nazis.

In all, some thirty people drowned trying to reach Sweden. An equal number took their own lives.

TEN

THE BATTLE CONTINUES

IN MID-SEPTEMBER 1943, shortly before the attempted roundup of the Jews, a group of seven leaders from different resistance groups met in Copenhagen to form Denmark's Freedom Council. The Council filled the political vacuum left by the resignation of the government. Its purpose was to coordinate the work of the varied resistance groups to fight the Germans in every way possible. Its ultimate goal was to return freedom, democracy, and independence to Denmark. Within a short time, Danes looked to the Freedom Council for political direction.

Although the council publicly announced its formation in early October, it remained, as it had to, an underground organization. When Council members were captured by the Germans, other resistance leaders took their place. The Council's reports were published in the illegal press, broadcast over the BBC, and printed on handbills that were distributed throughout the country.

The Council's first full proclamation was about the persecution of the Jews:

> The Danish Freedom Council sharply condemns the pogroms the Germans have set in motion against the Jews in our country. Among the Danish people the Jews do not constitute a special class but are citizens to exactly the same degree as all other Danes....The Council calls on the Danish population to help in every way possible those Jewish fellow citizens who have

not yet succeeded in escaping abroad. Every Dane who renders help to the Germans in their persecution of human beings is a traitor and will be punished as such when Germany is defeated.

It was a call to action, and Danes responded tirelessly. On October 7, the end of the first week of persecution, some 700 people escaped. The high point of the rescue was two days later, when 1,400 made their way to Sweden. Swedish records show that by the middle of October, 6,670 refugees had arrived there. By the end of November, approximately 7,600 people had fled Denmark across the Sound.

October 1943 was Denmark's turning point in the war. The need to assist the Jews energized a population that viewed the Germans with increasing anger, but had not yet focused that anger in any sustained form of mass protest. Aage Bertelsen, a schoolteacher in Zealand, responded to the crisis in a way typical of many Danes. He and his wife helped to organize a group that assisted hundreds of Jews to Sweden. In a book he wrote about the rescue, he noted that he had at first supported "the so-called collaboration policy." But by the summer of 1943, he found himself increasingly sympathetic with the escalating acts of sabotage. "So the dark night of the first and second of October meant a personal dawn. From now on there was no doubt or uncertainty possible. In the face of these open acts of atrocity, insanely meaningless, it was not a question of one's viewpoint. Action was the word."[14]

That was true for many others as well. In reviewing the events of that time, Jørgen Kieler believes many of today's historians

> …make a mistake. They try to disconnect the rescue of the Jews from the rest of the resistance. It all belongs together. We had the twenty-ninth of August, which was a revolution that showed that Denmark was not going to be a German ally. The resistance movement gained enormous public support by the twenty-ninth of August. But how long this excitement would have lasted, nobody knows. Then, one month later, the Germans do this most stupid action, the persecution of the Jews. Now there was no doubt any longer. You could not in any way be of any other opinion than that of the resistance.

The lasting effects of the rescue effort on the resistance were many. Scores of people remained active, participating in a variety of actions. In addition, the sailing routes to Sweden set up during the rescue remained open. Intelligence information, resistance people, mail, Allied officers who had been shot down, government officials, money, and weapons—all flowed between the two countries. The network of routes and couriers expanded and became permanent.

After October, incidents of sabotage continued to rise. Factories throughout Denmark that produced goods for the Nazis were bombed. Railroad sabotage interfered, at times significantly, with German troop transports. Even La Tosca, the restaurant frequented by Germans and the scene of Leif Vidø's weapons theft, was bombed.

By the end of the year, Hitler was furious at the increasing sabotage in Denmark. It was not enough, he concluded, to execute saboteurs, for that only turned them into martyrs. Instead, he ordered reprisal killings. Five Danes must die for every German soldier or informer killed. The well-loved poet and playwright Kaj Munk was the first victim of these reprisal killings. His brutal murder in January 1944 stunned the nation. By the end of the war, nearly five hundred Danes had been killed in such reprisal actions. Many of the killings were carried out by Danish Nazis.

By mid-October, after most Jews in Denmark had escaped to Sweden, Jørgen Kieler resumed his sabotage activities. The resistance group, Holger Danske (HD), was down to two people. Some members had been killed and some caught by the Nazis. Others had escaped to Sweden. One of the two remaining Holger Danske saboteurs, whose cover name was "John," became the leader of Jørgen's group. They called themselves "Holger Danske 2."

As sabotage actions increased, so too did the number of stikkers. Jørgen and the others watched with increasing dismay the Germans' success at bribing some Danes to betray others. One terrible day John was shot by the Gestapo, and then imprisoned and tortured. He had been betrayed. Once again for Jørgen and the others the resistance had to fight a two-front war: this time against stikkers as well as Germans.

More sabotage, Jørgen urged. That, surely, was what John would have wanted. From November 1943 until February 1944, HD2 succeeded in blowing up twenty-five shops and factories that produced weapons and food for the Germans.

When his group destroyed the Varde Steelworks factory in Jutland on December 12, 1943, the *New York Times* had a front page story about the action. The *Times* reported incorrectly that "forty to fifty Danish patriots" were involved. Actually, only Jørgen and nine other men were responsible for the sabotage.

The Varde action saved many lives, for it meant that the RAF did not have to bomb the factory. For Jørgen, saving Danish lives was one important reason he believed in sabotage actions. When the British had tried to bomb the Burmeister and Wain shipyard in the center of Copenhagen in January 1943, they had missed the yard but killed a number of people. In December, the Kieler group blew up the shipyard with no deaths.

In February 1944, Jørgen, his brother Flemming, and two other members of HD2 were betrayed. They were arrested after a sabotage action at two factories in Jutland. Jørgen's friend Peer Borup was killed. Jørgen was shot in the neck, beaten, and imprisoned in Copenhagen. Other members of the group escaped to Sweden, but one, called "the Flame" because of his red hair, stayed underground in Denmark. He now set about catching Danish traitors. When he himself was finally caught by the Nazis a few months later, he took a poison pill to avoid arrest.

Within a short time almost everyone in the Kieler family was arrested. Jørgen's sisters Elsebet and Bente had tried to escape to Sweden, but were betrayed. Jørgen's father was arrested at his home in Jutland. Only his mother and youngest sister remained free.

In the Copenhagen jail, Jørgen was interrogated repeatedly from his arrest in February until the end of May. Throughout that spring, the Gestapo regularly executed prisoners. With each new

Jørgen Kieler was betrayed by an informer and arrested in February 1944 during a sabotage action.

act of sabotage, they executed resistance people waiting on death row. John, from the Kieler group, was killed in April.

Jørgen and the HD2 members were next, but their execution was postponed twice. Jørgen wasn't sure why. One possibility, he thought, was that the Gestapo agent in charge of their case knew the war was lost. Or perhaps, Jørgen speculated, he even had some sympathy for a family with two brothers on death row, and two sisters and the father behind bars. But at last the delay was over, and a date was set for their executions.

Then, twenty-four hours before their scheduled killing, outside events intervened. Copenhagen was engulfed in a general strike, martial law was again declared, and all executions were put on temporary hold.

Before the executions in Denmark resumed, Jørgen was deported to a German concentration camp. There had been sixteen people in his group. By the end of the war, half were dead.

The Riffel Syndikat factory, producing machine guns for Germany, is destroyed by sabotage.

∾

The summer of 1944 Copenhagen was ablaze with resistance. June 6 for most of the world was D-Day. In Denmark, it was also "Globus" day, the day dozens of resistance fighters from BOPA blew up the Globus factory on the outskirts of Copenhagen. The factory produced parts of the V-2 rockets that were pounding London. Børge Thing was one of the leaders of this action.

Then, on June 22, 1944, the Riffel Syndikat factory, which produced machine guns for the Germans, was blown up. The damage was the most extensive of any sabotage action in Denmark.

∾

Inger had decided to go into Copenhagen. She didn't like to travel to the city, with all the disturbances going on, but she was meeting a friend she hadn't seen for a while. She sat by the train window reading a newspaper, but her mind wandered from the articles. She had listened intently to the BBC radio reports earlier in the week. The Allies were advancing through Europe, and bombings and sabotage had certainly increased in Denmark.

It was thrilling, she thought, that the Germans seemed to be on the run, yet also terrifying. The Nazis in Denmark were getting tougher. Bobs was underground most of the time now, and she knew one of these days she'd have to take the kids to the country to get away.

BAM! The sudden explosion shook the train. She jumped up, startled, and looked out the window. Everyone in the train rushed to her side of the car. They were just passing the harbor before arriving at the station. Smoke filled the air in great circling billows of black.

"Riffel Syndikat!" someone shouted. Of course, she thought. The resistance has blown up the machine-gun factory! All along the car, windows were thrown open and everyone crammed together to look out.

Inger found herself cheering and shouting along with everyone else. Hurray! she cried out, her voice lost among dozens. Suddenly, loud cracking shots pierced the air. The joyous shouts abruptly stopped. The Germans were shooting at the train. Inger dropped to the floor. Dozens of people crouched beside her in the center aisle. Bullets shattered windows and ricocheted off the railroad siding. It seemed to Inger that the shooting lasted a long time. In fact it was over in minutes, for the train hadn't stopped at all. Miraculously no one was hit.

≈

Two days later, the Schalburg Corps, at the direction of the Germans, bombed Tivoli Gardens. It was almost like an attack on the king. The king stood for Denmark. In the same way Tivoli, more than just an amusement park and gardens, was Copenhagen in the summer. It was a small center of peace in the storm of war. It was the joy of light summer nights after the long winter darkness. Now Tivoli was yet another victim of the war, and Danes were enraged.

Sabotage continued to escalate, and German reprisals became increasingly violent. There were more shootings of civilians, arrests, executions, deportations. Instead, however, of terrorizing the general population, the German actions had the opposite effect. On Monday, June 26, 1944, Copenhagen answered with a massive strike that virtually shut down the city. Within days the Germans turned off the gas, water, and electric supply. On Saturday, they completely blockaded the city, cutting off all food supplies. The Germans, proclaimed the Freedom Council, planned to starve Copenhagen into submission. The standoff ignited a cycle of strikes and rebellions throughout the country.

On Sunday, July 2, Copenhagen officials and trade and industrial council representatives urged the workers to end the strike. The Freedom Council, however, continued to support the strike until the Germans met certain demands, such as removing the hated Schalburg Corps from the streets of the city and ending the Germans' random shootings of innocent civilians. The Germans finally agreed. On Monday, July 3, the Freedom Council issued the following proclamation:

> These concessions from the Germans are so significant, that the Freedom Council does not hesitate to urge the population…to resume work….This peoples' strike has shown the Germans that the Danish people will not let itself be threatened or terrorized….The peoples' strike was only a prelude to the decisive fight that is imminent.
>
> To make all preparations for this decisive fight…for the struggle for peace, freedom, and independence, that is the Danish liberation movement's most important and paramount task.

In the weeklong uprising, 664 Danes had been wounded and 87 killed.

The previous summer's collapse of the government and the efforts to rescue the Jews had brought about a change in the Danish police. In the first years of the occupation, although some had helped the resistance in covert ways, the vast majority had remained neutral. Many saw themselves as a buffer between the population and the Germans. A few were definitely pro-Nazi.

In the early days of the resistance, some activists had viewed the Danish police as simply an extension of the "collaborationist" policy. Their distrust had turned to anger in late 1942. The Special Operations Executive (SOE), the British covert group working with all European resistance movements, had trained Danish agents to return to Denmark to start sabotage operations. The leader of the Danish group was Michael Christian Rottbøll. He had fled to Sweden, made his way to England, and in April 1942, had parachuted back into Denmark. On September 26, he was killed in a shoot-out with the Danish police.

After the summer and fall of 1943, however, the Danish police in large numbers reflected the change in the population at large. Many refused to carry out German orders. Others became actively involved in helping the resistance. By the fall of 1944, with the increase in sabotage actions and the nationwide strikes, the Germans had had enough. On September 19, in a surprise raid on police stations throughout the country, the Germans carried out a mass arrest of the Danish police. In their place, the Germans organized the Hilfspolizei (HIPO), an auxiliary police force made up of Danish Nazis, many of whom were former members of the Schalburg Corps.

Some two thousand Danish policemen were deported to the concentration camps at Dachau and Buchenwald. Six thousand went into hiding, many making their way to Sweden.

~

More were coming that evening, Bobs told Inger. Then he went down to the basement to set up. Inger had lost count of all the policemen who had come through the house. Since the Gestapo arrests, thousands were in hiding all across the country. Many were trying to get to Sweden, and they needed false I.D. papers. Bobs and his friend Poul were photographing them for their new identity cards.

The fact that Bobs was a professional photographer specializing in portraits was the perfect cover. He had every reason to have a darkroom in the cellar. Since he usually photographed people in the living room, however, he continued to do that. He wanted everything to look as normal as possible.

Inger covered the windows with blackout cloth and moved a small table and two chairs. Bobs came upstairs and set up the backdrop screen, lights, tripod, and camera. Within a short time, Poul arrived with negative plates to develop along with the ones Bobs would take that evening. The two had been working for over a week, almost round-the-clock, to get the photos ready for the false papers. They'd deliver the prints to a courier, and the rest was in someone else's hands.

The doorbell rang, and the first of many policemen came in. Bobs and Poul worked for several hours, and then finished earlier than they had expected. Inger was in the kitchen when she heard them leave.

About half an hour later there was a quick, incessant ringing of the doorbell. When Inger opened the door, Knud rushed in. He was a member of Bobs's group—really too young, Inger thought, to be involved. But he had apparently lied about his age when the group was first formed.

He was out of breath. "I—I—We were caught!" he stammered, waving a pistol about.

"What do you mean?...And stop pointing that thing!" Inger said, horrified. She took him into the dining room.

After several tries, Inger finally got the story out of him. He and a friend had been caught stealing weapons. They'd been arrested and were being driven to Gestapo headquarters. The car had crossed railroad tracks, and Knud saw his chance.

"I jumped out and rolled down the embankment and ran through the woods to you," he said, proudly, waving the gun again.

Suddenly, it fell from his hand to the floor. They both stared at the dent it had made. Thank God it didn't go off, Inger thought.

"What are you going to do if the Germans come here after you?" she asked.

"Shoot my way out!" he said with bravado.

"Knud, are you crazy? You can't do that. I have two small children here!"

Inger heard the key in the door. When Bobs came in, she took him aside. He agreed immediately that the young man had to be taken away.

"You're going to Sweden," Bobs said, as he walked back to the dining room. "And now I have to take your picture."

That night, Bobs took Knud to another house. Three days later, the boy was on a boat with his new I.D., headed for Sweden.

Inger worried that some of the resistance people were a little too daredevilish. The risk-taking, the narrow escapes—all pumped up their adrenaline. But this wasn't just a great adventure. This was deadly serious.

After the war, they learned that Knud's friend had been shipped to Theresienstadt.

Collecting weapons remained an important job for resistance groups. Saboteurs needed arms and equipment, and so did the underground army that was in training for the possibility of war being fought on Danish soil. Tage Seest's group was one of two in Copenhagen making weapons. Some weapons were smuggled in illegally from Sweden, and some were stolen in Denmark, from German supplies. The largest number, however, came from the British and later American airdrops. About 7,000 containers of weapons were parachuted into some 300 sites throughout Denmark.

In 1944 and 1945, if the Germans caught Danes who were collecting weapons, they either sent them to concentration camps or executed them immediately. One family group that had collected weapons from RAF drops was brought before a German tribunal in Copenhagen, tried, convicted, and executed.

Erik Jensen knew it could be dangerous to be in the resistance. At a school assembly one morning, the headmaster had announced that an older boy from the school had been executed for his under-ground activities. It was a moment of sadness and silence Erik remembered for a long time.

In the summer of 1944, when Erik was sixteen, he was an apprentice at a small country store that sold lumber, grain, gro-ceries, and other supplies. One day a worker in the store asked him, "What is Z in Morse code?" Erik didn't remember.

"But you can do Morse code, right?" the man insisted.

"Sure," said Erik. He had, after all, been a boy scout. "Why?" he asked. The man explained, and that's when Erik became involved in the resistance. He was one of the youngest in his cell. The group needed him to signal RAF bomber planes that they were at the right site for a weapons drop.

Erik had no idea who or how it was decided where the drop would be. His small cell had about a dozen members. They were informed only that a drop would take place sometime during a par-ticular week. The one certain piece of advance information was the location.

Most people Erik knew listened to the BBC at 6:15 each evening. At one point in the program an announcer might say, "And tonight we have special greetings to Peter, Hans, Nils, and Emmy." Before he was in the group, Erik had heard these announcements and never thought much about them. Now he knew they were code words. When his group heard a particular code name, they knew the action would be that night.

Erik and a few of the other workers had rooms above the store. They all ate together. As they came in for dinner one evening, Erik said quietly to his friend, "We have to make sure the radio is on." This week there was to be a drop in their area. The man nodded. Erik began to eat his cheese sandwich. This was his first weapons action, and he was anxious for it to happen.

"And now special greetings for Henrik, Kirsten..." Erik took another bite. "Lars..." Erik froze. That was it! LARS! He didn't hear another word of the broadcast, and he didn't look at his friend. He just tried to continue eating as if nothing had happened.

To aid the resistance, the British Royal Air Force drops weapons canisters and supplies by parachute.

When he finished, Erik started upstairs. His friend left at the same time and whispered, "Come to my room in a little while."

Within half an hour the group had assembled. Everyone was dressed in black. They divided into twos and headed separately to a big farming estate, the site of the drop. They still didn't know the time, but they had been told it was usually around midnight.

They waited in the darkness. At last the bomber circled over the town. Erik signaled, and the plane turned back and flew over the field. The small group quickly set up wind lights, indicating the direction of the air flow. Since the weapons canisters were dropped by parachute, the bomber had to determine when to release them, taking wind direction into account.

Erik stared up at the plane. He watched the bomb gates open. A small square of light shone down from the inside of the plane. Then eighteen tubes, six feet long and eighteen inches wide, came hurtling down, each on its own parachute. They hit the ground with a crash. Erik and the others rushed to remove the parachutes and load the canisters on to waiting trucks.

Hours later Erik and his friend returned to the store. That night they'd been lucky. No German patrols in the area. Erik fell into an exhausted sleep.

～

By the end of 1944, the Nazis had so much information about the Danish underground, that resistance leaders asked the British Royal Air Force to bomb the Shell House, Gestapo headquarters in Copenhagen. The RAF had successfully bombed Gestapo headquarters in Aarhus. The Shell House, however, contained the largest collection of Nazi files on resistance activists, and the resistance wanted it destroyed.

At first the English refused. The Germans kept important Danish prisoners on the top floor and their files on the lower floors. It was virtually certain the prisoners would all be killed in any raid. But the danger to hundreds in the resistance movement was greater, and at last the RAF agreed.

The Royal Air Force, flying very low, bombs the Shell House, the headquarters of the Gestapo in Denmark.

The British planners made models of the surrounding Danish landscape and all the buildings within a kilometer of the target. One of the official Danish newspapers "unofficially" helped. *Berlingske Tidende* ran a series of articles on the architectural designs of different Copenhagen buildings, one of which was the Shell House. The paper was smuggled to Sweden and then to London. And so in a seemingly innocuous feature article, the RAF was able to get up-to-date photos and architectural drawings of the building.

On March 21, 1945, three waves of Mosquito bombers and fighters left England headed for Denmark. To avoid German radar, they flew low over the North Sea, almost skimming the surface. Water sprayed their windows.

Thirty-two prisoners were locked up on the top floor of the Shell House, including two members of the Freedom Council. The RAF pilots had been instructed to shoot at the base of the front of the building. The hope was that some of the prisoners might be able to escape down the back stairs.

Ebba Lund and her brother-in-law had just walked out of the Shell House, when they heard the planes overhead. "They were flying so low," Ebba said, "we could see house rooflines above the planes. Looking up and seeing a building higher than a plane is quite dramatic!"

Within minutes the attack began. Six Danish fire engines arrived at the scene. They waited as long as they could before attempting to douse the flames. They wanted any files still in the building to burn up. When German fire trucks arrived, one of the Danes yelled, "Explosives!" and the Germans fled. The Danes then rushed to the back of the building, hosed it down, and helped escaping prisoners.

The bombing of Shell House was a remarkable success. Of the thirty-two prisoners, twenty-six escaped. Only six died. Within half an hour the building was in ruins.

Though most of the Gestapo files burned, some were dispersed by the explosions and lay scattered in the streets. One of the resistance fighters whose life was probably saved by the Shell House bombing was Bobs Peschcke-Køedt. Not long after the bombing, he received a strange package from someone who knew him. It contained pages from his Gestapo file that had been found in the street.

The success of the bombing was marred by a terrible tragedy. One of the bomber planes in the second wave of the attack struck a railroad tower near the Shell House. The plane crashed into the nearby French School, which burst into flames. When the third wave of planes swooped low for the attack, they saw the smoke near the railroad yard and released their bombs on the school, thinking it was the Shell House. Over a hundred children were in attendance that day. Eighty-three children, twenty nuns, and three firemen died.

∼

Not long after the war was over, the Johansens came with their daughter Emmy to visit the Peschcke-Køedts in Charlottenlund. Anne and Emmy were the same age, now six, and they hadn't seen each other much during the war. As they headed into the bedroom, chattering away, they looked like two ordinary little girls with nothing on their minds but fun.

It was Saturday, and Anne was telling Emmy she was glad there were two days without school. She didn't much like her school, she said. "How about you?" she asked Emmy. The young girl grew silent. She then began to tell Anne a strange and remarkable story.

Emmy was a student at the French School. It had been bombed, she said to Anne, who listened intently. You were allowed to speak only French at the school, all day long, and Emmy sometimes got really tired of it. That day she had pretended to be sick, and her parents had let her stay home. She paused and shivered. Many of her friends had died that day in the fire.

"But it was the English who bombed!" Anne said, trying to understand. "Isn't that right?"

"Yes," Emmy answered.

They both sat in silence. It was almost impossible to understand that Emmy would never see her friends again. Suddenly, Anne felt the world was a lot less certain a place than she had always thought.

ELEVEN
THE CONCENTRATION CAMPS

FORTY MILES NORTH OF PRAGUE in Czechoslovakia is the town of Terezín, built as a fortress at the end of the eighteenth century. When the Germans annexed Czechoslovakia, they renamed the town Theresienstadt. A short distance from the town is a smaller fortress, which served the area's rulers and then the Nazis as a military prison.

In November 1941, the Nazis began to use Theresienstadt as a concentration camp. Jews from Czechoslovakia, Germany, Austria, Holland, and Hungary were imprisoned there. Most were sent from Theresienstadt to the gas chambers at Auschwitz, where nearly all were murdered. By the end of the war, more than 140,000 people had been imprisoned at the camp. Over eighty percent of them died, a quarter of them while still in Theresienstadt.

The town was designed to hold about 7,000 people, half soldiers, half civilians. During the war, the Nazis crammed in some 60,000 Jewish prisoners. At first, the prisoners shared the town with Czech civilians. The Germans, however, needed more room for all the Jews they were shipping to the extermination camps. By mid-summer 1942, the town's inhabitants were forced to relocate, and all of Theresienstadt became a Nazi concentration camp.

Almost from its beginnings, the Nazis planned Theresienstadt as

Theresienstadt concentration camp

a transit camp, a way station for "transports to the East," as they were known to the inmates. These transports were death caravans to Auschwitz, where most of the prisoners were gassed upon their arrival.

In Theresienstadt, prisoners slept, sometimes two, three, or four to a bunk, in different buildings and barracks. Mattresses made of straw shoved in paper sacks were riddled with bedbugs and lice. Paper-thin blankets were encrusted with dirt. Filth in the latrines was almost beyond description, and diseases, as might be expected, were rampant. Epidemics of diphtheria, scarlet fever, and typhus at different times raged through the camp. Many prisoners suffering from malnutrition died of "natural causes." That is, they starved to death.

It often seemed arbitrary who lived or died. Prisoners could be shot or hanged for greeting an SS officer in an "improper" manner, such as not raising their caps quickly enough. All Jews had to wear the yellow Star of David. An inmate could be killed if the star were not sewn on properly. These were often called "political crimes," and prisoners were sometimes sent to the little fortress for their punishment. Fear was an ever-present emotion, a part of daily life.

More than half the children in the camp, many of them orphans, lived in special barracks. The rest stayed with their mothers or fathers. Education was officially forbidden, but sometimes went on in secret. Children were, however, allowed to participate in "cultural" activities. In fact, thousands were forced to learn and perform in an opera. They sang, to the Germans' great amusement, about an uprising against oppression. Within days of each performance, the children were put on transports to Auschwitz.

The painter Friedl Dicker-Brandejsova taught hundreds of children to draw and paint. Although she and most of the children were sent to their deaths at Auschwitz, many of their paintings survive and can be seen today in Prague and at the Theresienstadt museum. In all, some 14,000 children passed through Theresienstadt.

There was hardly any medical care in the camp, although many prisoners were eminent European doctors. The one medical service the Nazis did provide was a delousing facility. Insect-borne diseases were so rampant, delousing of prisoners was necessary, the Nazis reasoned, to protect German soldiers stationed at the camp.

Their arrival in Theresienstadt marked the first time Danish Jews had to wear the yellow Star of David.

When the Germans began their assault on the Danish Jews in the fall of 1943, they shipped those caught to Theresienstadt. Yet even here the Danes fought for their people. From the moment the Danish Jews arrived at the camp, Danish officials pressed the Germans for information about them. Some half-Jews had been deported, and the Danes tried to have them returned to Denmark. They continually requested permission to send packages to the inmates. Along with the International Red Cross, they demanded access to German concentration camps to see what was happening to Danish citizens. Actually, Danish officials never made a distinction between prisoners who were Danish citizens and those who were stateless refugees, halutzim, or League children. Their concern extended to all who were sent to the camps from Denmark.

In light of the International Red Cross and Danish pressure, the Germans began work on an elaborate plan to deceive the world about conditions in their camps. They chose Theresienstadt as a "model camp," and the only camp the Red Cross would be allowed to visit. The "beautification" of Theresienstadt was completed in the summer of 1944, and on June 23, 1944, the gates were opened to a representative from the International Red Cross and two Danish observers.

It was a date that would become a hideous Nazi joke. An orchestra greeted the delegation; newly painted and refurbished storefronts appeared to stock bountiful supplies of food; children in one of the children's homes were offered sardines for lunch, as they cried, "Oh no, Uncle Rahm [the camp commandant], not sardines again!" They, of course, had never been given sardines before, and were not allowed to eat them after the visit. The weak, sick, and disabled were hidden in barracks and lofts not shown to the delegation.

The visitors were assured there were absolutely no "transports East" from Theresienstadt to other camps. There had been, of course, transports before the visit, beginning in January 1942. And some 17,000 had been sent to Auschwitz to make the camp look less crowded during the inspection. Additional transports were resumed within weeks of the visit.

A small, selected group of elders, including Copenhagen's Chief Rabbi, Dr. Friediger, was introduced to the delegation. The day before the visit they had been warned they would be deported if they spoke to the visitors about the real camp conditions. One of the Danish delegates brought greetings to Rabbi Friediger and the imprisoned Danish Jews from King Christian X and Bishop Fuglsang-Damgaard. The Danish prisoners were deeply moved that the king and bishop had remembered them.

Most prisoners were confined to their barracks. The delegation passed a children's playground. A group of children, Birgit Krasnik among them, played with a large collection of toys. The toys were taken away the moment the delegation left. The Nazis made a film called *The Town the Führer Gave to the Jews*. Prisoners in the film appeared to be happy, sitting at cafes, eating at restaurants, attending concerts. When the film was completed, the whole "cast" was deported to the gas chambers. The Nazis even created paper money to make it seem that the town had a thriving economy.

The truth, of course, was that Theresienstadt, although not an extermination camp, was a concentration camp in which some people were killed; many died; some were beaten and tortured; and most were brutalized, starved, and humiliated.

~

When Birgit Krasnik and her family arrived in Germany, they were taken from the ship to a railroad siding. People all around Birgit were in shock. An old woman lay on a mattress on the ground, screaming. Her hands and feet were handcuffed, and she wore only a nightgown.

Birgit didn't know how many days or nights passed as they rattled through the German countryside, packed into a cattle car. Inside the car, it was dark, and the air was thick with the smell of fear, sweat, and urine.

Mrs. Krasnik was pregnant, and when the family arrived at Theresienstadt, Birgit and her mother were sent to live in a special house for pregnant women and mothers with small children. Birgit's father lived in a separate barracks for men. He had with him the dark blue hat with a silk band that he had always worn when he sang in the synagogue choir. In camp, he put it away. "I will take it out again when we go back home," he told Birgit.

All the grown-ups were supposed to work every day, but Mr. Krasnik urged his wife to try to get out of it. And so each day she'd say to the German soldiers, "I'm so sorry, but I can't go today. Birgit is ill, and there's nobody to look after her. Maybe tomorrow." In that way, she managed to avoid work for several months.

Birgit knew from hearing her parents talk that her father had to carry big stones from one place to another. That was his daily job. She could see the exhaustion in his eyes even as he would smile and give her a hug.

The Germans didn't want any new babies in the camp. If a woman was only a few months pregnant, they tried to get her to end the pregnancy. Mrs. Krasnik was four and a half months pregnant, but she and her husband decided to tell the Germans she was seven months pregnant. Perhaps that way they would leave her alone.

After four months in camp, a Nazi officer said to her, "According to our records you are now eleven months pregnant. How is that possible?"

Birgit's father, who was visiting the women's house at the time, said, "Yes, yes, in Denmark we go eleven months."

"Like elephants," the German officer said.

"Yes, like elephants," Mr. Krasnik answered.

For Birgit, nighttime was hard. She'd lie on the lumpy mattress and try to go to sleep as quickly as possible. Bedbugs came out at night. If Birgit fell asleep quickly, she wouldn't feel them biting her. During the night, Mrs. Krasnik would get up to pick them off Birgit's face. It was a battle she couldn't win. When she'd go back to sleep, more would come. Birgit awoke every morning bitten all over and swollen.

One morning when Birgit tried to get out of bed, she couldn't walk. The camp had a small field hospital that wasn't really a hospital at all. Prisoners who were doctors could usually diagnose what was wrong, but there was little they could do, for there was hardly any medicine and very little equipment.

When Mrs. Krasnik took Birgit to the field hospital, the doctor examined her and said, "Impetigo." Her legs were covered with a red rash and small pus-filled blisters. The infection and inflammation, the doctor said, were very bad. Birgit had a fever and couldn't tell what was happening. All she knew was that her mother rubbed something on her legs and then covered them with bandages. A little Danish boy, Birgit's age, also had impetigo. They were put together in the same bed, Birgit's head at one end, the boy's at the other, and both had their legs bandaged.

When Birgit began to get worse, the doctor said she had to have a blood transfusion to live. A makeshift system was devised, and Mrs. Krasnik's sister Paula twice gave blood to save her little niece. Ten days after the transfusions and daily bandaging, Birgit was able to walk again. A little wobbly at first, but at least she was alive and standing. After a while, the boy also recovered.

In February 1944, Birgit's little brother Preben was born. Two weeks later, Red Cross packages began to arrive for the Danes in the camp. Birgit's mother always said it was those packages with powdered milk and food that kept Preben alive.

But the little boy didn't have any clothing. Birgit's Aunt Rifka worked at a job sorting the clothes of people who had died. One day she came across a small pile of baby clothes. It was an automatic death sentence for anyone caught stealing from the room. Rifka knew this, but took the clothes anyway.

Birgit learned the word "transport." It terrified her. She knew it meant that people had to get on a train and go to the East. They never came back. She heard the grown-ups whispering about transports. Every time a transport left the camp, Birgit's parents and aunts wondered if they'd be next.

Not long after Birgit's brother was born, an SS officer told Mrs. Krasnik that Birgit had to live in a special children's house. Only one child was allowed to live with the mother in the women's house. Since the baby had to stay with Mrs. Krasnik, Birgit must go. Mrs.

Krasnik persuaded the officer to allow Birgit to return each night to sleep with her in the women's house.

And so every day Birgit went to one of the children's homes. It was really an orphanage for several hundred German Jewish children whose parents had been sent to the extermination camps. Birgit was the only child with a family that was still alive, and the other children resented her. She was glad to go back to her mother and brother every night.

One morning before he went to work, Birgit's father came to the women's house. "I had an awful dream," he said to his wife, his voice shaking. "I dreamt all the children at the children's house were put on a transport. In my dream I saw Birgit screaming from the window of the train as it pulled away. I tried to reach her, but I couldn't."

"You've been brooding about these transports," Mrs. Krasnik said. "That's why you're having these dreams. It doesn't mean anything."

Mr. Krasnik shook his head. "You must take Birgit out of there today and keep her with you. You must!" To calm her husband, Mrs. Krasnik made up some excuse and brought Birgit home.

The next day Mrs. Krasnik was ordered to go to work at the children's house. When she arrived, she was told to help the children pack up all their belongings. Later that evening the children were put on a train and transported to the East.

Birgit often played with a little Czech girl who lived in another building. One day her friend was taken to the delousing center. When she came back, all her hair was shaved off. The little girl sobbed uncontrollably. Embarrassed and humiliated, she tried to hide her bald head. Birgit found it hard to look at her friend. Then she remembered the blue hat with the red design, the hat the girl had given her as they stood on the dock in Copenhagen, waiting to board the ship to Germany.

When she offered her friend the hat, the little girl's face lit up, and she immediately put it on. Maybe it was a magic hat, Birgit thought, meant to help lots of little girls.

Weeks passed, and the little girl wore Birgit's hat day and night.

One day when Birgit went to her friend's house, the little girl and her mother were gone. Nobody would tell Birgit where they were. All they said was, "She's not here anymore." Birgit went back to her room and sat on the edge of her bed. She looked down at the yellow star with its six points sewn on her dress. It was on the left side, over her heart. In the middle of the star, it said *Jude*. She wondered if one of these days she, too, would have to leave on a transport.

≈

After the roundup of the Jews in Denmark, the German High Command tried to repair some of the damage to the relations between the two countries. Although the Nazis were the occupying force in Denmark, they still wanted and needed the cooperation of the Danes. One month after the roundup, during a November 1943 visit from Adolf Eichmann to Copenhagen, Werner Best convinced Eichmann to agree that Danish Jews in Theresienstadt would not be transported to other camps. The Danish Jews in Theresienstadt, however, did not learn of this until after the war. And so for eighteen months they waited in fear for a day that never came.

Danish Jews were not the only Danes to be sent to concentration camps. Resistance activists, thousands of Danish policemen, and other Danes the Nazis deemed "undesirable" were transported to Dachau, Buchenwald, Sachsenhausen, Neuengamme, and several smaller work camps. By the last year of the war, there were some 6,000 Danish prisoners in German camps working as slave labor, at least ten percent of whom died.

The transport from Denmark to the German camps was often a chilling experience. One Danish survivor of Neuengamme has written about his group's arrival at a train station in Germany:

> The stares of hate that the civilian population sent us, we prisoners could compare to the women salivating and knitting in the first row by the guillotines in the French Revolution. So ice-cold and without mercy did they look upon us prisoners from a neighboring country, standing there like in

a cattle show. That we were humans made of flesh and blood did not seem to affect them in the slightest. Here they had a perfect opportunity to show their power. They almost fought, old and young, men and women, to get to the front to spit at us, so that they could show us what was in store for us.[15]

Conditions in these camps were similar to those in other concentration camps: hunger, cold, disease, humiliation, fear, and death were the main components.

∾

When Jørgen Kieler and other Danish prisoners arrived at the Neuengamme camp in late 1944, they were told to strip and shower. Then other prisoners shaved them from head to toe. The new arrivals picked through a pile of clothing left over from prisoners who had died.

Neuengamme was a work camp. New prisoners were greeted by an SS officer who explained that although they came in through the entrance gates, they would leave a different way. He pointed to the tall chimney of the crematorium that spewed forth smoke day and night.

But Jørgen didn't stay at Neuengamme. Within days, he was sent on to the camp at Porta Westfalica. At Porta, the inmates were put to work building a multistory factory deep inside a mountain to protect the factory from Allied bombing. The prisoners blasted and dug out underground tunnels, roads, and halls in which the Germans set up electronic equipment stolen from Holland.

Jørgen had arrived at Porta with a group of 200 Danes. Within six months, about half of them were dead. Because of his medical school training, at first Jørgen was put to work in the sick ward. But he was interested in saving lives if at all possible, or at least in reducing pain and misery. The Germans, on the other hand, did not want to waste time. They wanted a factory built. Jørgen didn't last long at the job. He was then sent to work in the mountain.

At night the prisoners returned to bunk beds. Forced to sleep two to a bunk, it was not unusual to awaken in the morning to find your fellow prisoner lying dead next to you. Porta was a work camp with one of the highest death rates for a camp of its kind. The work was backbreaking, and lasted at least twelve hours a day. Food was scarce. Most prisoners lost between sixty and eighty pounds. By the end, thousands had died from exhaustion, starvation, and disease.

Although not officially a death camp, there were occasionally punishment killings. One prisoner who had tried to escape was hanged, and other inmates were forced to walk by the corpse. Another prisoner was killed in a public murder by one of the camp officials, who tied him up and hit him with a hammer throughout the course of a day.

Worse than the physical terrors, Jørgen feared that moment when a prisoner gave up. You can see it in their eyes, he thought. When you no longer dream, when you no longer remember the faces of the people you know and love, when you are filled with a blankness—that's when you are a *Muselmann*, as the Germans called it, the walking dead. Every prisoner knew a Muselmann would die within a short time. To hang on, Jørgen knew—that was the battle.

At last the Red Cross packages with food began to arrive at the end of 1944. Now there was hope, Jørgen thought. If he could just hang on.

TWELVE
NEARING THE END

SWEDEN PROVIDED A SAFE HAVEN for Danes, some 18,000 of them, including the Jewish Danes. The Swedes registered the refugees at reception centers, where they assessed peoples' needs. Swedish groups helped people find housing and provided other necessities. Young men were often sent to work camps, frequently logging camps in the vast northern forests.

In the refugee camps there were special schools for Danish children, with books smuggled in from Denmark. Some people moved out of the refugee camps fairly quickly and into their own apartments in different cities. Swedish agencies helped them find jobs as well as housing.

Some refugees organized a military force like the "waiting groups" back in Denmark. Sweden, however, was neutral, and so Danes could not officially set up an army there. Rather, in early 1944, they formed what was called a "police battalion," and later became known as the Danish Brigade.

There are no exact figures, but it is estimated that the Danish Brigade had between 5,000 and 7,000 men. The Brigade was a volunteer army, with about 750 Jewish members.*

Leif Vidø always remembered the date—September 17, 1943. That day he and his resistance group fled to Sweden. They had been distributing illegal newspapers and stealing weapons from German soldiers. And they had tried to find a sabotage group to join, but had been unsuccessful.

*Volunteers were not registered by religious affiliation. The number of Jews was estimated, based on their names or known ancestry.

A Danish school in Sweden: Leo Goldberger standing at far left; Salli Besiakov seated fourth from the left

Leif was living outside of Copenhagen. One day during the state of emergency in the summer, several group members announced, "We've shot one of those swine!"

Leif knew exactly whom they were talking about. The light-green-uniformed SS policemen from the Baltic states. They were among the most brutal and hated of all the Nazis in Denmark. Leif's group was urged by resistance people to get out of the country, and quickly.

And so one evening, the group collected their weapons and went to the harbor in Copenhagen. They approached a ship that was scheduled to sail to Germany. They walked up the ramp, their guns in their pockets. When they found the captain, they brandished their weapons and demanded to be taken to Sweden.

"Dear friends," said the captain, smiling, "do me a favor and shoot out the lamp!" He was under contract to sail to Germany, but his heart was with the resistance. He brought out a bottle of brandy, and they all raised their glasses to a safe trip to Sweden.

Over the next five months, Leif lived and worked in several different places in Sweden. Then, in February 1944, he began training
with the Danish Brigade. The military exercises were long and hard.
One hundred and forty-four people started in his group, and forty-
four were left after three months.

Leif loved it. He enjoyed the rigor, but even more he relished
the idea of a Danish troop fighting the Germans. "I look forward to
having a real rifle, not our silly little pistols!" he told a friend.

Another date Leif never forgot was March 28, 1944. On that
day, having successfully completed his training, Leif Vidø became
an official soldier in the Danish Brigade.

Johan Legarth had helped many a downed pilot escape to Sweden. In
September 1944, when he was betrayed by a stikker for his work with
the illegal press, he too fled the country. Shortly after his arrival in
Sweden, he joined the Danish Brigade.

Leopold Recht, as a young Danish Jew, was happy to join the
Brigade. It was an official way to fight the hated Nazis. After he had
saved his little niece Jette from drowning during an escape attempt, his
family had at last made their way to Sweden. Within months, he, too,
was undergoing the hard military training.

And Lui Beilin, one of a handful of Jews active in the resistance,
also fled to Sweden with his family. In February 1944, he began training with the Brigade and held a leadership position with his group. As
a Brigade member, he was later involved in helping Jews who arrived in
Sweden from the concentration camps.

In 1945, in what has become known as the "Bernadotte action," thousands of prisoners were released from German concentration camps
before the end of the war and brought to Sweden. The operation was
named after Count Folke Bernadotte, nephew of the Swedish king
and vice-president of the Swedish Red Cross, who negotiated with
the Germans for prisoner release. Bernadotte, while helping to organize the release of the largest group of prisoners, in fact became

involved in the rescue operation well after it had begun.

The prisoner rescue operation was started by the Danes and Norwegians working independently of each other in late 1943. After the transport of 481 Danish Jews and 150 Danish communists to German concentration camps in October 1943 and subsequent deportations of resistance fighters, Denmark's Director of the Ministry of Social Welfare, Hans Henrik Koch, and several other directors pressed for the release of the prisoners. They organized mailings of food packages to the prisoners through private groups as well as the Red Cross, and coordinated efforts to help the families that remained behind.

Copenhagen city officials were also concerned about the Danish Jews who had fled to Sweden, ninety-five percent of whom lived in the city. They were, after all, Danes, the officials reasoned, and it was hoped they would return to Denmark as soon as conditions permitted. The city assumed responsibility for the affairs of nearly 2,000 Jewish families, paying bills (including mortgage payments or rents), renegotiating outstanding contract obligations, and storing furniture and valuables.

With the arrest and deportation to German concentration camps of the Danish police in September 1944, Koch and others pressed hard for the release of the Scandinavian prisoners. In December 1944, the Germans agreed to return "non-dangerous" prisoners, that is, those who were not communists, saboteurs, or resistance activists. The Danes rapidly assembled a fleet of cars, trucks, buses, and ambulances that drove to the Buchenwald concentration camp and picked up some 200 Danish policemen. They were taken to Frøslev prison, a Danish prison camp near the German border. During the next few months, more prisoners were taken from other German camps as well. Many were seriously ill and had to be transported to hospitals in Jutland. By the time Bernadotte and the Swedes became involved, the Danes already had a well-organized rescue operation.

Germany was losing the war. No one, except perhaps Hitler, believed otherwise. Heinrich Himmler, the head of the SS and overall commandant of the concentration camps, tried to negotiate a separate peace with the West in order to turn Germany's full efforts into the war with the Soviet Union. Behind Hitler's back, he held secret meetings with Bernadotte about the release of the Scandinavian prisoners. Himmler agreed to the transport of the prisoners to Sweden if Bernadotte would act as a go-between with the western allies.

In March 1945 Swedish buses and ambulances, all painted white with a huge red cross on the top, drove through air raids and bombings to the Sachsenhausen camp and brought back 2,176 Scandinavian prisoners. All the prisoners were brought to the Neuengamme camp, which became the coordination point. This Swedish activity lasted four weeks. Then the Danes took over. Swedish rescue workers had been hired for one month, but some chose to remain to work with the Danes. The operation was called "the action of the white buses."

Neuengamme was overflowing with prisoners. Hundreds died before the camp was closed, and the crematorium worked overtime to dispose of all the corpses. The Danish national railroad outfitted a first-aid train to go to Germany. In addition, volunteers drove some 120 buses and ambulances from Denmark to evacuate prisoners from Neuengamme as quickly as possible. Some crossed the border into Germany before the white paint on their vehicles had dried.

∽

When Jørgen Kieler heard the rumor about the white buses, he wondered if it were true. Exhausted and weakened by starvation and dysentery, he knew he couldn't last much longer. The Red Cross food packages had helped. But, still, he knew it was only a matter of time before he'd reach the end. When he looked at his comrades in the camp, he knew it was the same for them. Too many had already died. If the buses were coming, it had better be soon.

Then one day the Scandinavians at the Porta Westfalica camp were taken back to Neuengamme. Could freedom be near? No one knew for sure, but despair in camp was for the first time leavened with hope. The prisoners watched as transports of Danes and

Norwegians arrived from other German camps. Neuengamme was bursting at the seams.

One April morning, there were the white buses! Most prisoners had to be helped onto the buses, some even carried aboard. But they were on their way out of Germany.

The buses arrived at the border, and Jørgen sat at the window and stared out. He was back in Denmark. It was hard to believe. Outside, the Red Cross had set up a reception and disinfection center for the prisoners. Jørgen overheard two nurses talking, and he was stunned to realize they were talking about his mother.

"Look, there's Mrs. Kieler. She must be looking for her sons. Someone will have to tell her that they're both dead."

Jørgen climbed down from the bus. "Hello, Mama!" Looking at

The "white buses" transport Scandinavian concentration camp prisoners back to Denmark in March and April 1945.

her, he realized his mother was seriously ill. And it was extremely difficult, Jørgen learned, to travel long distances in Denmark at this point in the war. He was astonished that she had been able to make the hundred-mile trip. But then his mother had always been a tower of strength in the Kieler family.

It was April 20, Mrs. Kieler's birthday. "Happy birthday!" Jørgen smiled.

Mrs. Kieler caught her breath and hugged him. "And Flemming?" Jørgen pointed to another bus where Flemming waited to disembark.

Then he had to say good-bye. The prisoners were taken to the Frøslev camp for several days, and then on to Sweden.

In his negotiations with Bernadotte, Himmler had rejected the request to free any of the Danish Jews. That was simply unacceptable for this high-placed Nazi. Bernadotte accepted Himmler's decision without challenge.

Dr. Johannes Holm, however, did not. Dr. Holm, a Dane working with the rescue group, was determined to free his fellow countrymen. His plan was in fact quite simple. Bribery. First, he sent a Danish car and convoy of white buses to Theresienstadt. On Friday, April 13, the car arrived at the camp headquarters. The next day the buses pulled up.

In Denmark, Dr. Holm filled up his car with Danish delicacies — sausage, pate, beer, schnapps, butter, pastries — and drove to Gestapo headquarters in Berlin. He threw a private party for the Gestapo officer who was the German liaison with Bernadotte's headquarters. After many hours of drinking and eating, Dr. Holm convinced the Nazi officer to sign a piece of paper. It is quite possible the officer did not realize what he was signing. It was in fact an order authorizing the release of the Danish Jews from the Theresienstadt concentration camp.

Birgit Krasnik sat beside her mother on the bunk bed, watching. The other women in the room moved like little waves, rushing together in small groups, then rolling back apart, then grouping together again.

Something was happening, and the Danes seemed excited.

Suddenly her father walked into the room. He came over to the bed and took her from her mother. "I have something I want to show you," he said.

Birgit looked up at him. "You have your blue hat on."

"Yes," he said, "because there's something I have to show you."

He took her hand, and they walked outside into the street. "Can you see those white buses with the red cross?" he asked.

"Yes, papa."

"These buses are going to take us back to Copenhagen."

"No! No! I don't believe it," Birgit whispered. It was the transport she had always feared would come for them. She began to cry.

"You must believe it," Mr. Krasnik said. "That's why I'm wearing my hat. Don't you remember what I told you?"

But Birgit was too afraid to believe. That evening all the Danish Jews were called together and told to go to one of the camp buildings. Birgit became sick. She felt certain it was a transport, perhaps a different kind, but definitely a transport, and maybe they would be taken to another bad place.

After two days in the barracks, 425 Danish Jews were brought out through the gates of the camp on a convoy of white buses. Fifty-three Danes had died in the camp. A Theresienstadt orchestra played as the group left, and the other inmates waved, cried, and cheered, and prayed for their own deliverance.

Birgit stared at her father. He still hadn't taken off his blue hat. Maybe it really was true after all. Maybe they were going back to Denmark! Birgit slowly began to breathe easier.

The allies had been bombing Germany for weeks, and the buses had to make their way through a destroyed land. The remains of buildings stood like skeletons against a moonscape of devastation. Outside of Potsdam, near Berlin, the convoy pulled to the side of the road, and everyone scrambled off the buses and fled into the woods. Night was bright as day. Huge beams of light crisscrossed the sky, searching for the allied planes that hurtled down a rain of bombs. One survivor said "a true hell broke out over our heads."[16]

At last it was over, and the buses started up again. Two days after they left Theresienstadt, the convoy reached the Danish border. Birgit looked through the bus windows. Thousands of Danes stood in the streets of the border town waving Danish flags and cheering wildly. Danes had come home!

～

The remainder of the non-Danish Theresienstadt prisoners were freed in early May 1945, when the Russian army took control of the camp. The last Jew left Theresienstadt on August 17, 1945.

After the liberation of the Scandinavian prisoners, on April 21, 1945, SS chief Himmler agreed to allow the white buses to evacuate all the women prisoners at the Ravensbrück concentration camp—nationalities other than Scandinavian, Jewish as well as Gentile. Fleets of buses drove to and from the camp until the bombing prevented any further pick-ups. The camp commandant, realizing the Nazi defeat was near and seeking, perhaps, to lessen any future punishment he might face, sent a cargo train with the remaining women to Denmark. Thousands of women, many so weak no one knew if they would survive the journey, were transported from Germany through Denmark to Sweden.

～

One afternoon in Sweden Lui Beilin was taken aside by his Danish Brigade training leader. "You must take a crew and go immediately to the school gymnasium to set up a 'hotel'."

Lui was puzzled. "What do you mean?" he asked.

"Women from a concentration camp are coming, and they will have to live there until we can find other places for them."

Lui left immediately. He checked on the supplies he would need, and then organized a group of men into work crews. Hour after hour without break they stuffed large paper sacks with dried grass. At last they had a thousand mattresses.

Lui stayed at the school while his men went down to the dock to wait for the women. As the boat neared the shore, hundreds of women crowded on the deck. Suddenly they began to scream, "It's a trap! It's the Germans! It's a trap!" The Danes were wearing green

Swedish uniforms, but to these women, they looked like Nazi soldiers in green.

Suddenly one old woman began to shout, "They're Danes!" She must have seen the red and white Danish flag on their caps, the men later realized.

Many of the women were too weak to walk and had to be carried off the boat and to the "hotel." When they arrived at the school, Lui learned they were Hungarian. One of the women spoke to him in German, since he didn't speak their language. She said of the Nazis, "We were *holz*, wood for their ovens."

The next day a Swedish priest came to welcome the women. He wandered through the hall and came back to Lui. "I understand Hungarian, but many of these women are not speaking Hungarian," he said. "I think they are speaking Yiddish. Do you know anyone who can speak Yiddish?"

"Yes," Lui said quickly. "I can."

The women were sitting and lying on the floor of the large sports hall. The priest spoke to them in Swedish and Hungarian, welcoming them to Sweden. Then he turned to Lui.

Lui stood looking around the hall. It was a *nes*, a miracle, he thought, that these women had survived. He stood there in his uniform, with the Danish flag on his hat, and said, "Sholem Aleichem!" Women throughout the hall began to cry. He added, "A *hartsikn barukh habo!* A heartfelt welcome!"

And then Lui began to cry.

THIRTEEN
LIBERATION AND BEGINNINGS

IN THE LAST WEEKS of the war, the Germans frantically sought to hide the evidence of their war crimes throughout Europe. Slave labor camps were emptied as quickly as possible, and the killings and cremations intensified at the extermination camps. But the Germans also sought some last-minute victories. In Denmark, particularly after the bombing of the Shell House and the destruction of Gestapo files, the hunt for resistance fighters intensified.

❧

Bobs Peschcke-Køedt spent much of the last year of the war underground. His cover name was Harold Jensen, a great joke his family thought. "Harold Jensen" was the name of a famous aquavit drink, and Bobs did not like aquavit. Sometimes he would arrive at the house on his bicycle wearing fake glasses and a mustache. Bonnie and Anne knew not to say anything to him if they were on the street. Inside the house he was the father they knew, but outside he was Harold Jensen, a nearsighted, mustached stranger.

In the last year and a half, Inger also sometimes went underground with the children. She and Bobs knew that some wives had been arrested in order to learn the whereabouts of their husbands.

Despite reputed German efficiency, the Nazis didn't seem to know about the summerhouse. And so in early July 1944, after witnessing the sabotage destruction of the Riffel Syndikat factory, Inger took the children to their summerhouse on the coast near Elsinore. They lived across from a farmer who was a Nazi sympathizer, but at least they were away from the sabotage actions in the city.

Inger and the children remained through the summer and into the winter, and they huddled to keep warm in a house built only for summer use. Peter had been born in the spring, and the three children and Inger all slept in one bedroom. The house had a little wood stove in the kitchen and one in the living room. That was all the heating. There was no indoor plumbing. Only an outhouse.

When Inger got up in the morning, the side of her bed was covered with ice. She'd leap into boots and a big coat and rush into the kitchen to start up the wood stove to make the house a little warmer for the children.

Then at last it was spring. The BBC reported all the Allied bombings of Germany. Everyone said the war was essentially over. But German soldiers still shot at Allied planes that flew over the Sound. Because the house was high on a hill, the strafing passed right overhead. And there were still German soldiers everywhere. Only now they seemed to be all young boys and old men, nervous and jumpy as the war neared its end. Everyday in the papers there were stories about murders of both resistance people and stikkers.

In early May, Bobs telephoned to say there were rumors the war would end very soon. He didn't think it would be safe any longer in the country house. There were many Danish Nazis as well as Germans in the area. They both decided she should return to the city.

Inger hired a taxi, and with the three children inside and all their belongings strapped to the top of the car, they drove back toward Copenhagen. The road was filled with cars, suitcases strapped on top, all traveling away from the city. Who's doing the right thing? she wondered.

～

At 8:30 P.M. on May 4, 1945, people all over Denmark were tuned in to the BBC news broadcast. As announcer Johannes Sørensen was reciting the news of the day, he was handed a telegram. He interrupted his report to read the two short sentences:

Danes celebrate the announcement of the German surrender to Field Marshal Montgomery.

FIELD MARSHAL MONTGOMERY ANNOUNCES THAT ALL GERMAN FORCES IN NORTHWEST GERMANY, HOLLAND, AND DENMARK HAVE SURRENDERED. THE SURRENDER BECOMES EFFECTIVE AT 8 O'CLOCK TOMORROW MORNING.*

Danes across the country poured into the streets, laughing, crying, shouting, singing. The war was over at last, and Germany had been defeated!

The next day people thronged in the streets of Copenhagen. Many rode their bicycles into town, flags and flowers decorating the handlebars. That evening candles lighted windows all across the

---

*The unconditional surrender of Germany was on May 7, ratified at Berlin on May 8, but May 5 was the day of surrender of German forces in Denmark, and that, of course, is the date Danes celebrate as the moment of their liberation.

country as people tore off all the black curtains that had darkened their lives for five years.

But even though the war was over, for a few days the fighting continued. German soldiers holed up in a barracks outside of Copenhagen at first refused to surrender. The underground "waiting groups" were activated, and in a senseless shootout one Dane was killed. Finally the Germans conceded defeat.

The last holdouts were Danish Nazis. Hated by their countrymen, they had nothing to go back to, and so they fought to the end. In a particularly fierce battle in north Zealand, they were at last defeated. The armored car that now stands in front of the Danish Resistance Museum in Copenhagen was used in that final battle.

Enormous crowds in downtown Copenhagen greet Field Marshal Montgomery on May 12, 1945.

The Danish Brigade returns home.

The Danish Brigade returned to Denmark from Sweden right after the German surrender. They arrived in Elsinore and marched down the coast road to a wildly enthusiastic welcome from Danes who lined the streets and filled the balconies all along the route. But even amidst the joy there was gunfire. As the Brigade marched through Copenhagen, they were fired on from the rooftops by Danish Nazi snipers.

The celebrations in Copenhagen went on for days. British Field Marshal Montgomery rode through the crowd-filled streets of Copenhagen. Some joyous onlookers, including Inger Peschcke-Køedt, climbed the lampposts to celebrate the end of the blackest years in recent memory. When King Christian drove through the city in an open car, normal life, Danes thought, was beginning again.

At last the Germans marched out of Denmark, leaving their weapons at the border. For many, the sight of the long lines of soldiers, departing bedraggled and defeated, was the true moment of liberation.

For others, there was yet another moment that said "liberation."

∾

Bibber Peschcke-Køedt and his underground resistance unit patrolled the area near the American ambassador's house just outside of Copenhagen. During the war, the German high commandant Werner Best had taken over the building for his private residence. One day, Bibber's unit received a telephone call.

"Please come and pick me up," the voice said. It was Werner Best. He wanted to surrender officially to Danish authorities, for he feared rogue freedom fighters would kill him now that the war was over.

The van with Bibber's unit pulled up to the residence. Bibber and several others rode outside on the running boards. Werner Best was taken into the van and driven to the Copenhagen jail. Bibber wore the helmet he had trained in for so many months. And now he

Dr. Werner Best, former high commandant for Denmark, at his arrest

Just after the German surrender, Tage Seest, first row center, and members of his group wearing the resistance armbands

also wore the official resistance armband that had been distributed to all resistance fighters. Although the Germans had surrendered, the arrest of Werner Best closed the book.

In mid-May 1945, Danish Jews poured out of Sweden and returned to Denmark. Some were forced to find new housing, since their homes had been taken over by people who wouldn't leave them. Most, however, found their belongings intact, just as they had left them when they fled or were arrested eighteen months earlier. Many homes and apartments had been cleaned and painted, and neighbors greeted the returning Jews with fresh flowers and well-cared-for pets.

Thousands of Danes had fought to save the Jews of their nation, and they had largely succeeded. Constant pressure from the Danish government had even kept the imprisoned Danish Jews from the Nazi gas chambers. But as remarkable as the rescue was the welcomed return. *"Velkommen til Danmark!"* And with that, the Jewish Danes came home.

Another fate, however, awaited the Danish stikkers. The resistance had compiled lists of collaborators. Some 15,000 were arrested, and 13,521 found guilty. Seventy-eight were given death sentences, forty-six of which were carried out.

Not long after the German surrender, Danes in Copenhagen experienced a most joyful moment. As they stood in the old and beautiful town squares, streetlights and neon signs, dark for five long years, were at last turned on.

SOURCE NOTES

All public documents cited in the text without source notes are either in the author's possession or are reprinted in Leni Yahil's *The Rescue of Danish Jewry*, one of the most detailed histories of the rescue operation.

[1] Reprinted in William Shirer, *The Rise and Fall of the Third Reich*, p. 681.

[2] Ronnie S. Landau, *The Nazi Holocaust*, p. 298.

[3] Danish Rabbi Marcus Melchior relates this story in his autobiography, *Darkness Over Denmark, A Rabbi Remembers*, p. 106.

[4] Ib Nathan Bamberger described what he called the "characteristics of the typical Dane" this way in his book, *The Viking Jews: A History of the Jews of Denmark*, p. 11.

[5] Quoted from William Shirer, *The Challenge of Scandinavia*, p. 236.

[6] The full telegram is reprinted in Yahil, *The Rescue of Danish Jewry*, pp. 138–139.

[7] Hans Hedtoft described his encounters with Duckwitz and Jewish leaders in Aage Bertelsen's book, *October '43*.

[8] Knudsen's story is told by Harold Flender in his book *Rescue in Denmark*, pp. 54–55.

[9] The phrase is Yahil's from her book, *The Rescue of Danish Jewry*, p. 188.

[10] There are several slightly different English translations of the bishop's letter. See Flender, p. 69; Leo Goldberger, ed., *The Rescue of the Danish Jews: Moral Courage Under Stress*, pp. 6-7; Yahil, pp. 235-236.

[11] *Life*, November 28, 1960, p. 101.

[12] Eyewitness account quoted in Yahil, *The Rescue of Danish Jewry*, pp. 184–185.

[13] This survivor has recorded his recollections on a tape that can be heard as part of a permanent exhibit on the rescue operations in the Resistance Museum in Copenhagen.

[14] Bertelsen, *October '43*, p. 25.

[15] From Erik Lindstrøm, *Afdansningsballet* ("The Last Dance"), pp. 205–206. Trans. by Anne Koedt (unpub.).

[16] Jytte Bornstein, in her book, *Min rejse tilbage* ("My Journey Back"), p. 172. Trans. Anne Koedt (unpub.).

WHO'S WHO CONTINUED

LUI (LEIB) BEILIN: During the war, Lui wrote articles for the underground press. He and his family fled to Sweden when the Nazi roundup began in October 1943. After he returned home with the Danish Brigade, he worked as an editor/journalist. He has also written for radio and television programs in Danish, Yiddish, and Hebrew. Lui and his wife, Ebba, live in Copenhagen.

SALLI BESIAKOV: After the war, Salli returned from Sweden to finish his education. He played jazz piano in Copenhagen to earn money while he studied for a degree from the Royal Academy of Art. After graduating, he worked in several architects' offices until 1956, when he opened his own architectural business. He has won more than thirty prizes for his designs of various public buildings. Salli lives in Copenhagen and has written numerous columns for Danish newspapers on many subjects, including his wartime experience.

BENT BOGRATSCHEW: Bent returned to Denmark from Sweden on his tenth birthday. "It was the best gift I ever had." Shortly thereafter, the family changed their name to Bograd. For many years, Bent was a buyer for a major Copenhagen department store, and then he opened his own clothing store. One day, nearly fifty years after the war, an elderly lady came into his shop. She was the woman who had hidden his mother, sister, and little brother on the night of the roundup. Bent has been very active in the Jewish Community and for a time served as president of the organization. He and his wife, Miriam Ruben Bograd, live in Copenhagen.

LEO GOLDBERGER: When his family's first plans for escape to Sweden fell through, Leo's father, Cantor Goldberger, took a train to Copenhagen to try to borrow money for another escape attempt. On the train a Christian woman recognized him from a concert performance and, seeing his distress, asked what was wrong. When he explained, she said she would "take care of everything," and told him to be at the train station within a few hours. True to her word, someone was there with money and instructions, and the family made their way safely to Sweden. In 1952 Leo emigrated to America. He has written and edited several books about the Danish rescue of the Jews during the war. He is a professor at New York University, on the advisory council of the Anti-Defamation League Braun Center for Holocaust Studies, and a member of the board of directors of the Thanks to Scandinavia foundation. Leo lives in New York City.

ERIK JENSEN (name changed for reasons of privacy): Sometime after Erik and his group collected weapons dropped by the RAF, Danish Nazis came looking for him. Everyone in town who was asked about him protected him, although they knew nothing about his activities. Even the teller in the bank said to him, "Mr. Jensen, if you need another place to sleep tonight, I have a guest room for you." The Nazis dropped the search. The parachutes attached to the weapons canisters that Erik retrieved were made of triangular patches of silk. When the war was over, everyone in his group got to keep one of the parachute pieces. Erik made his into a tie. "Not a great tie," he says, "but one filled with lots of memories." Erik moved to the United States in the 1960s and has his own business.

JØRGEN KIELER: Nearly everyone in the Kieler family was involved in the resistance, and most of the Kielers were captured by the Nazis. Miraculously, everyone survived. It took, however, several years for Jørgen and his brother Flemming to recover from illnesses contracted in the concentration camps. Jørgen became a doctor and is internationally known for his cancer research. He has also written historical papers about the Danish resistance and the Holger Danske group of which he was a member. He is currently at work writing a historical memoir about the war and the resistance movement. Jørgen and his wife live in Rungsted Kyst, north of Copenhagen.

BIRGIT KRASNIK: When Birgit and her family returned from Theresienstadt, her grandparents found their home exactly as they had left it, with the Rosh Hashanah dinner table still set. For many years Birgit worked for Danish television programs. Today, Birgit Krasnik Fischermann is the chair of the Theresienstadt Society, a group of former prisoners. "Because you've survived, you have an obligation to tell stories from that time. You have to tell how you remember it." Birgit speaks to school children throughout Denmark and travels with teachers and groups of young people on trips to concentration-camp sites. She and her husband, Salo Wassermann, live in Copenhagen.

JOHAN LEGARTH: Johan was at his brother's house when the Nazis came to arrest him. He had been betrayed by a stikker for his activities printing underground newspapers. He escaped out a window and fled to Sweden, where he joined the Danish Brigade. After the war, the stikker was tried for collaboration with the Nazis. When Johan returned to Denmark, he completed his schooling in trade and commerce. For several years, he worked in Greenland. When he came back to Denmark, he opened up an arts supply and paint shop. Since the war, Johan has not visited Gilleleje, the scene of the tragedy. Johan and his wife live on the coast, north of Copenhagen.

EBBA LUND: Ebba received her degree in chemical engineering after the war and spent a year doing research in immunology in the United States. She later worked in Sweden on research projects about polio and then returned to Denmark to teach. She became head of the Department of Virology and Immunology at the Royal Copenhagen Agricultural University. Throughout her active career, she has served on many committees and has been a member of Denmark's Ethical Council. Ebba and her husband lived in Copenhagen. Ebba died in the summer of 1999.

ANNE PESCHCKE-KØEDT: Six years after the war was over, Anne and her family emigrated to America, where she finished her schooling. She is an artist and has designed record covers, book jackets, and sets for theater productions. Anne was active in the civil rights, peace, and women's movements, writing numerous articles on women's issues. Anne now lives in New York City and is a children's book writer and artist.

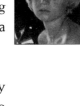

BOBS PESCHCKE-KØEDT: As a resistance leader, Bobs was offered a military commission after the war, which he declined. He and his family then moved to America in 1951, where he became "Bob" and simplified the family name to Koedt. In 1956 he moved to Wyoming to supervise the building of several of the complexes at the Grand Teton National Park. For many years he was a leading architectural designer in Jackson Hole, Wyoming, and built many homes in the valley. Bob died in 1992.

BONNIE PESCHCKE-KØEDT: Bonnie finished her schooling in America, moved to Canada, and worked as a documentary producer for the Canadian Broadcasting System. She also wrote a book and many articles about women's issues. As an independent documentary filmmaker, Bonnie has produced a number of award-winning films on women, the environment, and the arts. Bonnie Kreps lives in Jackson Hole, Wyoming.

INGER PESCHCKE-KØEDT: Inger has lived in a log cabin in Grand Teton National Park in Wyoming for nearly forty-two years and has been active in the environmental and women's movements and in local civic affairs. At age eighty-two, she helped bring the Anne Frank exhibition to Jackson Hole and began to speak to school classes about her wartime experiences, "not just about the painful times, but to see what can be learned to free us from prejudice. I tell the kids that a thousand years ago the Vikings killed people all over Europe. Now Denmark's a peaceful country. Things can change. It's the future that's important." Inger lives in Jackson Hole, Wyoming.

RENÉ (BIBBER) PESCHCKE-KØEDT: Bibber and his wife, Ditter, emigrated to America in the 1950s. They settled in California where they raised a family and were very active in the civil rights movement. For many years, Bibber worked as a sales representative for a California company. Since his retirement, he and his wife return to Denmark most summers and live in a little country house that was part of his family's home. Bibber has kept the full family name.

DORA RECHT (THING): Before the war, Dora Thing taught a kindergarten class and then worked for a government agency until she escaped to Sweden in 1943. In Sweden she started a kindergarten school for Danish refugee children. Within a few years after her return to Denmark, she began teaching again and continued to teach on and off for many years. After her husband, Børge, died, she worked for a Copenhagen government agency until her retirement. In a moving event fifty years after the end of the war, Dora was reunited in a radio broadcasting studio with both the young woman who had thrown her infant daughter Jette overboard during their first escape attempt and the dentist who helped her in her successful escape to Sweden.

MIRIAM RUBEN: Miriam and her family escaped to Sweden in early October 1943, but a cousin of hers had a different kind of escape. As a year-old infant, he was separated from his mother when she was hiding in a hospital ward. Taken by a priest, who didn't know the child's name, he was brought up by the priest and his family and given a new name. Her cousin was reunited with his family at the end of the war. Today Miriam Ruben Bograd is married to Bent Bograd and lives in Copenhagen. They have a summerhouse not far from the stables Miriam slept in when hiding from the Nazis.

TAGE SEEST: After the war, Tage resumed his university studies, graduating in

1947. "As we had been locked up in our tiny country during the war, I was possessed by the idea of seeing the world." And so he got a job as an engineer for a company that sent him to Venezuela. After two years, he started his own company there, selling machinery. In 1961 he and his family returned to Denmark where he worked as a top executive in several different companies. Tage and his wife, Ele, live north of Copenhagen, in Holte.

BØRGE THING: Børge went underground in 1942 and remained in hiding until the end of the war, all the while actively engaged in resistance activities. In 1944 he became the head of BOPA, one of the main resistance groups. At the end of the war, as a recognized resistance leader, he was offered an army commission, which he accepted. In 1955 he left the army and began a career in business, becoming the manager of a large firm. He died of illness at age fifty-four.

LEIF VIDØ: In early May 1945, Leif returned to Denmark with the Danish Brigade and was involved in some of the last skirmishes of the war. In the summer of 1945, he joined the British Army and was stationed near Hamburg, Germany. "It was a pleasure," he said, "to be one of the occupying forces in Germany." When he returned to Denmark, he earned a teaching degree and then a Master of Arts degree in Danish and English. For many years, he and his wife traveled extensively around the world. Leif died in 1999.

LEIF WASSERMANN: After the war, Leif's father worked for the Swedish government. Unlike most families, the Wassermanns remained in Sweden for many years, although they returned to Denmark every summer for several months. The first time the family returned, they found everything in their home exactly as they had left it. The only thing missing was the flagpole in their country house. "Someone had used it for firewood. Of course we forgave them." Leif came to America in the mid-1960s for graduate study. He worked in industry for several years before joining the foreign service. Today he is the consul at the Royal Danish Consulate office in New York.

SALO WASSERMANN: On the night of April 8, 1940, just hours before the German invasion of Denmark, Salo and his sister played in a piano recital at his teacher's apartment in downtown Copenhagen. It was a "quiet, lovely night," he remembers, the last truly peaceful night for five long years. He and several members of his family escaped to Sweden on October 4, 1943. His father and five other relatives drowned in the attempt. After the war, Salo returned to Denmark

and completed his education. He became the chief accountant in a dental equipment factory. Today Salo and his wife Birgit Krasnik Fischermann live in
Copenhagen and have a summerhouse not far from where Salo sailed to Sweden
that dark October night.

SELECTED CHRONOLOGY

(Bold face text refers specifically to events in Denmark)

1/30/33	Adolf Hitler becomes Chancellor of Germany.
9/15/35	German Reichstag passes Nuremberg Laws restricting Jewish activities and legal status. Over the next years, more restrictive laws follow.
3/11/38–3/12/38	German troops march into Austria.
9/29/38	As a result of Munich Pact, part of Czechoslovakia is ceded to Germany.
11/9/38–11/10/38	"Kristallnacht" (Night of Broken Glass)
5/30/39	**Denmark and Germany sign a non-aggression pact.**
8/23/39	Germany and Soviet Union sign a non-aggression pact.
9/1/39	Germany invades Poland.
9/3/39	Britain and France declare war on Germany, and World War II begins.
11/23/39	Polish Jews forced to wear yellow Star of David. Within a year, Star of David is introduced in all of the countries under German control except Denmark.
4/9/40	**Germany invades Denmark and Norway.**
5/10/40	Germany invades Holland, Belgium, and France.
6/22/40	France surrenders to Germany, leading to establishment of pro-German Vichy government in the south of France.
9/27/40	Japan joins Germany and Italy as an Axis power.

6/22/41	Germany breaks non-aggression pact and attacks the Soviet Union.
11/25/41	**Denmark signs the Anti-Comintern Pact.**
12/7/41	Japan bombs Pearl Harbor, and the United States enters the war. Within a few days, Germany declares war on the United States.
1/20/42	Wannsee Conference in Berlin formulates Nazi plans for the "Final Solution" of the "Jewish Problem": All European Jews are to be killed.
Summer 1942	Large-scale deportations of Jews from throughout Europe to concentration camps.
9/26/42	**King Christian X replies tersely to birthday telegram from Hitler, triggering the "Telegram Crisis."**
11/4/42–11/5/42	British General Montgomery defeats German General Rommel at El Alamein in Egypt.
11/5/42	**Werner Best, the new German high commandant of Denmark, arrives in Copenhagen.**
2/2/43	Germans surrender to Soviet troops at Stalingrad.
May 1943	German forces driven from North Africa.
8/28/43	**Werner Best hands Danish government an ultimatum. Danish government resigns in protest.**
8/29/43	**General von Hanneken imposes martial law. German forces march into Copenhagen. King under house arrest at palace.**
9/8/43	**Werner Best sends a telegram to Berlin saying the time has come to deal with the Jewish Question in Denmark.**
9/11/43	**Best tells shipping aide Georg Duckwitz of plan to transport Jews to German concentration camps.**

9/17/43	Hitler approves of plan to round up Denmark's Jews.
9/28/43	Duckwitz informs Danish Social Democratic Party leaders of planned roundup of Jews October 1 and 2.
9/29/43	Day before the beginning of Rosh Hashanah, Rabbi Melchior tells congregation of planned roundup of Danish Jews.
10/1/43–10/2/43	Germans and Danish Nazis carry out manhunt for Jews. Thousands of Jews go into hiding.
10/9/43	Fourteen hundred Jews, the greatest number on any single day, arrive in Sweden from Denmark.
November 1943	Eichmann visits Denmark. Agrees not to transport Danish Jews in Theresienstadt to extermination camps.
12/30/43	Hitler orders reprisal killings for acts of Danish sabotage.
6/6/44	D-Day. The Allies land on the beaches at Normandy.
	Danish saboteurs blow up Globus Factory outside Copenhagen.
6/24/44	Tivoli Gardens bombed, precipitating strike two days later.
6/26/44	General strike in Copenhagen lasts a week. Strikes in other Danish cities as well.
9/19/44	Germans arrest the Danish police. Two thousand are deported to concentration camps.
12/16/44	Battle of the Bulge begins.
1/28/45	Auschwitz–Birkenau concentration camp complex liberated by Soviet army.
3/21/45	The Shell House, Gestapo headquarters in Copenhagen, is destroyed by RAF bombing. RAF bombers accidentally hit the French School.
4/11/45	Buchenwald concentration camp liberated by American troops.

4/15/45	British troops liberate Bergen–Belsen concentration camp.
4/15/45	**White buses take Danish Jewish prisoners from Theresienstadt to Denmark and then Sweden.**
April 1945	**Danish and other Scandinavian prisoners brought from concentration camps on white buses.**
4/28/45	Dachau concentration camp liberated.
4/30/45	Hitler commits suicide in Berlin bunker.
5/2/45	Berlin captured by Soviet Red Army.
5/4/45–5/5/45	**German forces in Denmark, Holland, and northwest Germany surrender.**
5/7/45–5/8/45	Germany unconditionally surrenders. War in Europe ends.
8/6/45	United States drops the first atomic bomb on the Japanese city of Hiroshima, and three days later a second atomic bomb on Nagasaki.
8/14/45	Japan surrenders. World War II ends.

BIBLIOGRAPHY

I have included several Danish-language books and publications in this list because they were extremely useful to me in my research. And, perhaps a Danish-speaking person will read this book. In addition, I would like to note that Jytte Bornstein's book, *Min rejse tilbage*, is an extraordinary account of an eight-year-old's experience in a concentration camp. I hope that it will be translated into English for the wider audience it so richly deserves.

Abrahamowitz, Finn. *Gilleleje 43: A Play in One Act*. English version by Leo Goldberger. New York: Thanks to Scandinavia, 1993.

Bamberger, Ib Nathan. *The Viking Jews: A History of the Jews of Denmark*. Brooklyn, N.Y.: Soncino Press, 1983.

Barfod, Jørgen H. *Escape from Nazi Terror*. Copenhagen: A/S Forlaget for Faglitteratur, 1968.

Bertelsen, Aage. *October '43*. New York: G. P. Putnam's Sons, 1954.

Bogø, Dines, and Lis Thavlov. *Dragør og St. Magleby besat og befriet* (Dragør and St. Magleby occupied and liberated). Dragør, DK: Dragør Lokalarkiv, 1995. Translated by Anne Koedt (unpub.).

Bornstein, Jytte. *Min rejse tilbage* (My Journey Back). Copenhagen: Munksgaard/Rosinante, 1994. Translated by Anne Koedt (unpub.).

Elting, John R. *Battles for Scandinavia*. Alexandria, Va.: Time-Life Books, 1981.

Flender, Harold. *Rescue in Denmark*. New York: Simon & Schuster, 1963. Reprint, New York: Holocaust Library, 1991.

Goldberger, Leo, ed. *The Rescue of the Danish Jews: Moral Courage Under Stress*. New York: New York University Press, 1987.

Grayzel, Solomon. *A History of the Jews*. Philadelphia: The Jewish Publication Society of America, 1947.

Haestrup, Jørgen. *Panorama Denmark: From Occupied to Ally: Danish Resistance Movement 1940–45*. Copenhagen: The Press and Information Department, Ministry of Foreign Affairs, 1963.

————. *Passage to Palestine: Young Jews in Denmark 1932–1945*. Odense, DK: Odense University Press, 1983.

Hilberg, Raul. *The Destruction of the European Jews.* New York: Quadrangle Books, 1961. Reprint, New York: Harper Colophon Books, 1979.

Landau, Ronnie S. *The Nazi Holocaust.* Chicago: Ivan R. Dee, 1992.

Lindstrøm, Erik. *Afdansnings-Ballet* (The Last Dance). Copenhagen: Martins Forlag, 1983. Translated by Anne Koedt (unpub.).

Lowry, Lois. *Number the Stars.* Boston: Houghton Mifflin, 1989; New York: Dell, 1990.

Madsen, Benedicte, and Søren Willert. *Survival in the Organization: Gunnar Hjelholt Looks Back at the Concentration Camp from an Organizational Perspective.* Translated by Edith Matteson. Aarhus, DK: Aarhus University Press, 1996. Cambridge, U.K.: Cambridge University Press.

Melchior, Dr. Marcus. *Darkness Over Denmark, A Rabbi Remembers.* New York: Lyle Stuart, 1968; London: New English Library, 1973.

Rittner, Carol and Leo Goldberger. *The Rescue of the Danish Jews: A Primer.* New York: Anti-Defamation League Braun Center for Holocaust Studies, 1993.

Rittner, Carol and Sondra Myers, eds. *The Courage to Care: Rescuers of Jews During the Holocaust.* New York: New York University Press, 1986.

Rossel, Seymour. *The Holocaust: The Fire That Raged.* New York: Franklin Watts, 1989.

Shirer, William L. *The Challenge of Scandinavia.* Boston: Little, Brown & Co., 1955.

———. *The Rise and Fall of the Third Reich: A History of Nazi Germany.* New York: Simon & Schuster, 1960.

Silver, Eric. *The Book of the Just.* London: Weidenfeld & Nicolson, 1992.

Steinbeck, John. *The Moon Is Down.* New York: Viking Press, 1942.

Straede, Therkel. *October 1943.* Copenhagen: Royal Danish Ministry of Foreign Affairs, 1993.

———. "Operation 'White Buses,'" *The Resistance Fight 1940–45.* Copenhagen, 1998. Translated by Anne Koedt (unpub.).

Sutherland, Christine. *Monica: Heroine of the Danish Resistance.* Edinburgh: Canongate Press, 1991; London: Robin Clark, 1992.

Toland, John. *The Last 100 Days.* New York: Random House, 1966.

Werstein, Irving. *That Denmark Might Live: The Saga of the Danish Resistance in World War II.* Philadelphia: Macrae Smith Co., 1967.

Yahil, Leni. *The Rescue of Danish Jewry: Test of a Democracy.* Philadelphia: Jewish Publication Society of America, 1969.

INDEX

Page numbers in italic type refer to illustrations.